DISREGARDED ENTITY

Lessons Learned by a

15 Year Freelancer

RYAN VINSON

Disregarded Entity

www.DisregardedEntityBook.com

Published by VersusMedia LLC

First Edition First Printing

ISBN-13: 978-0692828519

ISBN-10: 0692828516

Printed in the United States of America

Cover image courtesy of Vector Frankenstein/Shutterstock

In memory of my cat Ramses, who lived to be 20 years old; he was my boss, best friend, and adventure buddy. Thanks for being the coolest cat a guy could ever want and keeping me from going crazy when things didn't go our way. I miss you every day.

Thanks to my parents for giving me the foundation and support to reach for the stars and follow my dreams no matter how crazy they may have seemed.

Contents

Introduction

I have been a self-employed freelance Internet consultant for over 15 years now. That's a long time to work in just my underwear. From time to time, I get asked questions by people who are interested in starting their own home-based business. And yes, I have also been asked before if I really work in only my underwear every day.

Some of these people were just like me in my early days. They wanted to do the exact same tasks they were currently doing, but quit their day jobs and work independently as freelancers. Not all of them worked in technology either. I have been asked these questions by writers, dog walkers, filmmakers, musicians, store owners, and craft designers.

They expect me to give a quick and supportive response about how amazing it is to chase my dreams and reject the conventional 9-5 lifestyle. They expect me to tell them how great it is to be able to roll out of bed whenever I feel like it and already be raking in piles of money before my first cup of coffee is finished. Sure, it is possible to get to this stage. With the right plan and perfect timing, anything is possible. But the kind of success that results in making consistent high income from home is rarely going to happen from the start. For most people, just focusing on how to obtain a stable income that can sustain you and your family should be the first goal.

Freelancing has become a hot topic around the Internet. There are estimates that as we continue further into this century, more and more people will be working independently as freelancers. The Internet has certainly made it much easier to work anywhere you want. Freelancing is not just for designers and software developers anymore. Translators, teachers, doctors, nurses, craftsmen, and musicians are current examples of careers that are starting to benefit more from the freelance world.

To some, freelancers appear to be less serious about their careers and may be sorely lacking in the necessary level of experience expected by corporations. I'll hold back my laughter on this misguided belief. I've had to wear so many different types of hats in my career, and been called upon to solve such a wide range of problems.

It is difficult for me to believe that someone working the same job day in and day out would ever run into as many unique and challenging situations as I have as a freelancer. If nothing else, I have learned so much crisis management from my years of freelancing that I could probably land a job in wedding planning if this ever gets boring. There have been far too many "Help me! The world is on fire!" moments for me to remember.

Many people are using the freelancer path to work remotely

as "digital nomads" in such popular destinations as Chiang Mai, Thailand, and Medellin, Colombia. This allows them to work on projects at higher rates, yet live in a cheaper location with a much lower cost of living than in Western cities.

I've personally just stuck to the USA. I may not be as nomadic as some of the "digital nomads", but freelancing has allowed me to travel and continue my work, as time permits. It certainly can be a little rough trying to answer work e-mails and take conference calls near midnight in Asia after a long day. Or waking up the next morning to a plethora of e-mail and voicemails. It's great that I am able to freelance, but it hasn't always worked out as smoothly as I wanted. A later chapter will delve more into the challenges of freelancing while traveling from my perspective.

As you can start to see, working for myself is not an easy topic for me to sum up in a sentence or two. Maybe others have had it easier than me, but the world of freelancing is an onion with many layers. After being asked questions enough times by people, I finally started to write down the most important tips and lessons I've learned. Then one day I decided to make an article about it. The more I wrote, the more I realized this would be better explained in a short book. So here we are.

This book contains personal experiences and my own opinions on how to handle being a freelancer and the complex challenges it presents. Some of the stories involve experiences with past clients that were not exactly ideal. I have not included any names, as I personally do not find that to be good business etiquette. Not everyone works well together—that's just how life is.

Trying to work with another person and perfectly understand their vision is extremely difficult. They may have a picture in their head of what they want you to do, but what comes out of their mouth may be something else entirely. What we hear and interpret from this may be something else entirely. We humans create some crazy misunderstandings with one another. Throw in a little bad luck and poor timing and things become utterly chaotic pretty fast.

Some of the situations in this book did improve over time, while others I just moved on from. Sometimes it just takes time for people to understand each other better. I know that at least a couple of clients in this book were ones that I had that moment where I wanted to never hear from them again. Yet over time, we started to better understand each other, and we've now had some very happy years of working together.

I always try my best to do exactly what the client asks, but I have learned from past experiences to know when to say "enough". For each of us, that moment may be different. Business reputation is important to me, but so is my personal dignity.

Burning bridges is something that I never want to happen with a client, but just like in other areas of life, things don't always turn out the way we want. All we can do is learn from these experiences. That's the general purpose of this book—to inform you of the important freelancing lessons I learned through my own misadventures. I hope that by going into detail about my own personal experiences and methods, you'll learn a thing or two about how to run (and maybe not run) your own self-employed freelancing business.

Let me make it as clear as possible by saying that this is not a book about how to get rich quick. I, myself, am not rich by any means. This book simply contains lessons I've learned from my own experiences as a self-employed person, and I thought that these lessons might be able to help someone else too. Maybe you have already experienced many of these situations. If you have, then I tip my hat to you. Hopefully, you will still find some of the key points in this book useful. While this book is about me starting a technology-centric small business, I am certain that a number of these lessons are also useful to people in other professions. As small business owners, don't we all end up encountering very similar situations?

When I started my first business, I had absolutely no idea where to begin. There were plenty of self-help books available back then, but taking the time to read all of them was not an option for me. When you are already knee deep in business dealings, you can't stop to take the time to read about what you should have already been doing. I did manage to read some of them in my early days. I found that some books covered certain topics too thoroughly, but then left out key details from other important aspects of running a business. If I could have combined all of the books I read together, then I would finally have a clear-cut plan to follow in order to get the ball rolling.

By first starting this book as just a bullet list and then elaborating further on each point, I feel I was better able to explain what I have learned over the course of my turbulent self-employed career. With that said, let's get started.

CHAPTER 1

In the Digital Wild West of the 1990s

The Internet changed my life. It's crazy to think where I would be if the Internet never took off. It boomed and I seized what I could as a naive 18 year old living in the tiny US Midwestern village of Energy, Illinois. It was all such a whirlwind in the beginning. My life and everything around me was moving extremely fast. With so little life experience, I blindly made decisions based on instinct and raw emotion. The Internet was only in its infancy, so the level of information available online was very limited. We didn't have the ability to research topics like we do now. Gut instinct possibly meant more back then. Now you can just search online until you have enough information to make calculated decisions.

I first started creating websites back when dial-up Internet was king. Just hearing that screeching sound of the modem connecting was like a race car engine revving up. The louder it got, the more excited it made me. While still in high school, I remember seeing the movie "Hackers" at a theater in 1995 and wondering if that's what life was like for computer hackers. I was already a fan of Jolt soda, thought computers were fascinating, and much of the movie's soundtrack fit with my own musical taste. So then I wondered, could I be a hacker? To do that, first, I needed to understand what exactly being a hacker entailed.

My brother had already made pen pals with people from around the world using the Internet at his university. Between his interest and mine, we managed to convince our parents some time in early 1996 to let us pay for our own monthly Internet access. The door was now wide open for me.

Within several months, I became completely absorbed in learning how to write code. I landed my first official job in the Internet world just after graduating high school in 1996. I sat at a booth in a Sam's Club as an Internet subscription reseller, working for the very same dial-up company that my brother and I got our own Internet service from. This job allowed me to spend hours in front of a company-supplied computer and learn the ins and outs of how the Internet worked.

It wasn't exactly the busiest place to work, but that turned out to be a gift in itself. While most of my coworkers played video games or read books, I spent time chatting with people from around the world and furthering my ability to write code. This was a beautiful time of my life—I was at the forefront of a new frontier. It is amazing to think now about just how little information was on the Internet back then.

After about a year at the reseller booth, I was offered a position to work in Network Operations at their main headquarters. This was a massive jump for me to go from learning programming and Linux in my free time to working 30+ hours maintaining hardware and dial-up routers. To me, this is the job that moved me from casual Internet user into something that felt like a real career path. I spent most of my time at night sitting in the office monitoring all of the locations where the company's dial-up modems were available.

It wasn't a very busy job for me directly. If there was ever any major outage, my boss would jump online immediately and handle most of it. I was able to go on road trips all over the Midwest with other coworkers and learn how to replace dead modems. I usually just went along for the ride, though. I was much younger than everyone else, and quite the rookie, so I don't think they felt comfortable leaving things directly in my hands.

I guess they at least saw potential in me, though. In the end, I was a glorified security guard, just for dial-up modems. My job description essentially said: if something happens, call somebody else to handle it.

It was at this job that I began to hear stories of other coworkers who were getting offers in major cities for large amounts of money. This planted the seed in my head that I could possibly use this method to move onto bigger things myself.

My college grades continued to slip further and further because my attention was firmly focused on the Internet. Why bother with slow boring school when I could hop on the Internet train at any time? I was ready to take on the world. The Internet was here to stay, and I wanted to be a part of it. It was my ticket out to a bright future, full of great opportunities. I knew it deep in my bones. The Internet would change my life, I needed to be ready for anything.

CHAPTER 2

Spotting Alter Egos

During my time working at the reseller booth and chatting online, I connected with a girl in my age group from Dallas, Texas who needed a programmer for a business idea she had. She was backed and funded by her stepfather and his son (who was a network engineer). After some discussions about code, I was given the approval to start.

I now had my first unofficial client at the age of 18. I helped her set up a free chat service similar to the one she and I chatted on daily, yet with a few distinct differences. The biggest difference was that it allowed musicians to share their music with people across all of the chat rooms. This was a big deal before digital download services were available. It became popular worldwide pretty fast since there was very little competition. At its peak, this platform had about 100,000 chat rooms. It felt really amazing to watch people use something I had built and chat to each other in foreign languages all over the world.

The reality was that I was a big piece of this from a creative standpoint, but in the end, I didn't own any of it. It was cool to help someone else, but it would be even cooler to one day have my own business. For now, it was just fun to be part of something that was becoming pretty popular.

Now, the story starts to become a little weirder. I had first met this girl in a chat room devoted to industrial rock band Nine Inch Nails called "the Ninternet". Myself, along with hundreds of other individuals, all chatted daily in this room. I spent hours most days chatting with her about the chat service, our significant others, music, interests, and more.

The late 90s was the time of webmasters and webmistresses, and anybody who knew what a TABLE tag was could land a job. My hometown, located deep in rural America, had a population of roughly 1,100 people. The nearest major city was over 2 hours away and technology was usually slow to reach us.

I was growing more and more eager to move somewhere larger with better access to technology. It crossed my mind one day that if I took a job in Dallas where she lived, we could work to expand our chat service during my time off. So I scheduled an interview with a company in Dallas. About 2 weeks before I left, I came online and saw everyone in the chat room freaking out. She had been killed in a car accident by a drunk driver.

This girl was very heavily liked, and everyone in the chat room was devastated. People created digital memorials for her, and one person even wrote and recorded a song devoted to her. CDs were made for all of us. I believe there was even a makeshift virtual funeral service for her. It was emotionally draining and sad. Someone who I considered a very close friend - who I had shared many long chat sessions with - was gone. Yet I had never actually met her.

Sad and beat down, I decided to still travel to Dallas for my interview. A couple of my friends drove me to the nearest airport 2 hours away from our town and even waved me off from the terminal gate itself. It was certainly a different era. A quick security check and anyone could go in with you. I had never been on a plane before so my coach seat felt like first class to me. As soon as I landed, my life would change. I was already having my first subtle test. No one was there to pick me up at the airport in Dallas. It may not seem like a big deal now, but I was already pushing further outside of my comfort zone than I had ever been. I figured out how to use the shuttle phones in the front and get a ride to my hotel.

I spent one night out with the girl's stepbrother, a guy I had barely ever even communicated with before. Most of my communication was always with his stepsister. He didn't really say much about her, and I didn't really want to bring up anything to cause bad feelings either. Looking back, it felt like when a client comes into town. I was wined and dined and the evening ended with a handshake. Then I went back to my hotel.

It all just felt awkward. I flew home not really knowing what to expect.

I didn't end up getting the job, but that was okay. This was my first experience in a larger city with a corporate Internet company. I had never flown in an airplane or stayed in a hotel alone before. It was my first time out in the world and on my own. That fact was ultimately my silver lining. It had broken the travel seal for me. I could make it on my own in a big bad city. For someone from a small town in farm country with very little access to the outside world, this just confirmed to me that a move was possible.

After I returned home, her stepfather (who I only had a few previous chats with) was now the point person taking over the chat service. Over the next several months, I slowly became less involved in making decisions and transitioned towards just being "the programmer". The direction he wanted to go with it just never sat right with me. I slowly pulled myself out of the project. Something just didn't seem right.

In my free time, I enjoyed researching my own family genealogy, and I became familiar with using the Social Security Death Index to look up my own relatives. One day, I decided to look the girl from the chat room up. To my surprise, she wasn't there. I knew she wasn't his biological daughter, so I tried combinations of what I was told was her real father's last name. I even searched records of car accidents in her area. Nothing was popping up.

While I had seen plenty of pictures of her during the time we worked together, I was never able to speak with her on the phone. She had claimed to have had a serious throat injury as a little girl that made it painful for her to speak at all. I just accepted this as fact and we never spoke on the phone. It always seemed like an odd thing to me, but I didn't really care too much. I was young and building up lots of experience. That's all that mattered to me at the time.

This may sound like a fairly common story in our modern era, but the idea that someone would go to this extent online to act like someone else was not a common idea back then. I was in my late teens at this time, so I was probably a little more gullible in those days. But I had already met a number of other fellow chatters in the surrounding parts of the Midwest. Some were similar to themselves online and others were nothing like their online personalities. One of them, who I became real world friends with, still believes this girl never actually existed. It's possible she may have been a real person, but the stepfather may have been using her persona online.

My general theory is that I was getting too close to figuring out who she really was when I decided I would move nearer to her. If this was truly the case, I can only guess what my role for the stepfather was. I guess I should assume he wanted to sell the chat business off eventually and take all of the profit for himself. Ultimately, it didn't really matter to me. This person helped me pass hours of boredom at my reseller job. She gave me a task to focus on, thus helping me learn to code faster. Don't we all work better when we have a goal to achieve? A weird situation for sure, but this experience coupled with my real job helped me move on with my career.

Today we have so many methods of being able to verify that people are who they say they are. Nothing is foolproof, but it's much easier nowadays to do some detective work. This doesn't prevent people from creating an Internet image of themselves as being wealthier, smarter, or more handsome than they really are. We have all become experts at knowing which angles make us look best in our own pictures.

It's best to always be on guard with clients, especially newer ones. They aren't giving you the full picture. Some may even just be providing you the perfect angle to sell you their project. They might not have the connections they claim to have, nor the capital to pay you after the project is over. At 18, that entire situation was my first experience of working from home for a client. Without a doubt, the freelancer bug bit me during this situation; I wanted more.

It became clear to me that I wanted out of my small hometown. I was in college, but I was always being distracted by the Internet. I realized that this Internet boom was a quicker route through the education system than finishing college for me. It was 1999 and the Millennium was coming soon. So I dropped out of college, accepted my first real position, and moved away to Atlanta, Georgia. My life and view of the world would never be the same after this.

CHAPTER 3

How Not to Run a Business

At what I like to call my first real full-time job, I received the nickname *"The Human Sponge", because* I was always trying to soak up everything around me. City lifestyles and the day-to-day activities people engaged in were all very new to me. In some ways, I felt like I had come from a cave. Life in a small town with very little opportunity made me feel extremely far behind the people around me. I often felt embarrassed and somewhat stupid for not understanding topics they were discussing. My eyes were now opened, though, and I took everything in my stride as best as I could. Understanding city living and the routines that went with it was almost like a second job for me.

During the day I was learning how to work at a large company and at night I was doing my best to acclimate to this new situation. Before moving away from home, I had rarely dealt with true city traffic. Now, the sheer volume of commuters every morning made me feel like I was in a spaceship navigating my way through an asteroid field. I had barely ever driven at high speed in my entire life. Now, here I was learning to survive cruising down the highways every single day.

I had also grown up with a very simple diet. 'Meat and potatoes' sums up what most of us ate on a daily basis. Every now and then, we might venture out to something beyond that, but it was a rarity to eat different food. I had no idea what sushi was like when I was first introduced to it (you eat it raw?). Most of what I knew about popular culture and city living came from movies. Eventually, I would learn just how much of that was blown out of proportion to make movies more interesting.

I'm glad I made this move when I was young, despite the fact that it was very exhausting. Weekends usually couldn't come soon enough. Sitting at home with my newly adopted cats from the local animal shelter made for a great weekend. I was a serious kid, though, and I wasn't going to ruin this chance I had been given. I always made it a point to keep an ear open and absorb everything the upper management at my new job discussed with each other.

The tech industry was booming so much that I could easily apply for a job somewhere else if I was tired of my current job. But deep down inside I just really wanted to become my own boss. My time working on the chat service gave me such a nice taste of being in full control. Its quick success also gave me that rush that many startups feel when things are going well.

I might have been young, but at least I knew that this dream would not be easy. I knew that if I truly wanted to start my own business I would have to take chances. But first I needed to soak up as much experience as I could from the people around me who were already running a business. I would need to understand all of the pieces that make a business successful.

If my current job wasn't teaching me anything new, I would become antsy to move on to something new. My gut instinct was warning me about something, and I had to listen. So I decided to hop jobs for a while to learn as many different areas of business as I possibly could. Not just programming, but business and sales skills as well. Without the financial ability or time to easily get an MBA, I figured the next best thing was *field experience*. With the boom in high gear, what was there to be worried about?

Like some of the more modern startups, many Internet companies in the 1990s weren't being run very well. Either they were growing too fast, venture capitalists were expecting too much too quickly, or the companies just had no real direction. Many of them were doing one or more of the following: overworking salaried employees, overspending on elaborate parties, renting unneeded office space, spending too much time in meetings without enough time for actual work, hiring people with no real purpose, or not really having any clear vision as to what their business should be. All examples of poor business practice.

Most people say that you should have a business plan for a reason. You have to know what you want to accomplish or you will never be able to reach a goal. It seems like common sense, but some of the companies out there clearly had no clue.

I also witnessed situations where the investors were controlling things too much and forcing people to make bad decisions. It's the age old problem. You need money to run your business the way you want it. Some people only want to invest money if they can have a say in the business. So the business owners decide to allow some input from the investors in return for the extra money. This extra input becomes a bigger problem every time they open their doors for additional money from new investors. Eventually, there is a "too many cooks in the kitchen" situation.

By the early 2000s, I was now in my early 20s and I had managed to bounce around the US working a few different jobs. With every job, came an increase in my salary. This was nice, but I was starting to see a terrible trend. With each position I took, I was actually doing less work. On the surface, that sounds great and I didn't want to complain. These companies were all being pumped full of cash that they really didn't need by investors who were now in control. So they were taking this cash and hiring employees that had no real purpose. These companies were full of big visions and dreams but they lacked common sense. To me, this is a telltale sign that a bubble was reaching its peak. It didn't take too much longer before many of my former employers were starting to shut down.

The Internet bubble was bursting. The market had become way too saturated and full of pointless startups. Investors were now tired of dumping massive amounts of money into ideas and never seeing a return. Several of my friends lost their jobs, and every week I wasn't sure if I would be next.

During this particular period of time, the tech industry buzz seemed to ripple from the larger cities down to the smaller ones. If the larger cities were booming, the smaller ones would be booming soon after. If the larger cities were losing jobs, the smaller ones would see the same thing in due course. In 2000, I could see the writing on the wall and decided to move from Los Angeles, California to St. Louis, Missouri to take one final position with a small web development company.

I hoped to absorb as much information as possible about running a small operation before time ran out and the bubble fully burst. Buy low, sell high was my theory. Start the company near the bottom of the bubble while living on the savings from my current job. Then I would have a functioning business of my own by the time the market would turn around.

That's the thing about trying to have business insight. You can research as thoroughly as you think is necessary and still not be 100% certain that now is the right time. Being young with no real commitments other than buying cat food made it easier to take this risk. There was always something in the back of my mind every time I spent money. That this money I was spending could be used more effectively towards building my own company. Each time I overspent, I knew I was damaging my own chances of success. I had seen what happened to a number of my employers who wasted their money on stupid stuff. I knew what

I wanted to do, so I decided to carefully examine how I spent my money. I had to make my choice: do it or shut up.

I consulted a local law firm where a friend of a friend worked. They suggested I create a Single Member Limited Liability Company (LLC), and then mark it as a disregarded entity on my tax returns. With the LLC, I would have some basic protection for my personal assets if I was to ever be sued. Things were now in motion.

CHAPTER 4

Feast or famine

I wasn't aware of the phrase *"catching a falling knife"* in those days, unfortunately. The general idea behind this metaphor is that you're grabbing on to something as it continues to fall further down. In business terms, you purchased something while its value was still falling. You should have waited until it hit the bottom or as close to it as you possibly could have. Then you pull the trigger and make your purchase. Choosing when to make that decision is something plenty of investors hope to learn how to master. There is no method 100% effective at solving the riddle of "when is the right time to buy?".

Many people will tell you their theories and formulas that are apparently sure-fire ways to know. Whether they are legitimate is another story. When it comes to business, you have to try and look for signs and signals that something is failing. Then you need to study the information available to determine if it will fall further or if the market is about to rebound.

I had read enough books about running one's own business, but reading and experiencing are two entirely different things. No matter how much you think you are prepared for something, you will never know until it happens. Nowadays, I firmly feel that real world experience far outweighs anything I could ever read in a book. You have to experience things directly to fully understand them. I would trade 20 book-smart individuals for a handful of experienced workers.

I felt that I had absorbed enough information from other people to know that there were significant dangers in running your own business. By trying to do this while having a salary, I could guarantee myself that I would have money while I continued my quest to becoming self-employed. But should I try to start a business right now while the Internet bubble was still bursting? Had the bubble fully exploded by now? Or was there still more to come?

During this time working at the small web development company, is when I set up my first official business and started moonlighting on my own web development projects. Many were from former bosses and past coworkers of mine. All were tiny projects but I had to start somewhere. I wanted to make a slow transition from employee to business owner.

I connected with a potential client who had several projects of their own that they were close to starting. I would basically be a subcontractor to another web company. That really didn't matter to me as I was young and eager to get some projects started. It was during one of my dinner meetings with these people that I first heard the phrase "feast or famine" being connected to running your own business.

For small businesses like mine who do not have access to a full staff team, we don't have a sales force who can help us constantly find new projects. Sometimes you get lucky and the projects are constantly flowing in. This is when you are having a feast. If your projects all dry up or you just can't seem to find anything, this is when you are having a famine. These famines were becoming more common for me as the bursting of the tech bubble worsened.

This company wasn't very big, and had maybe 4 full-time staff members. But one of the key guys in the company was heavily connected to a large company in the area. This meant they always had a funnel of work coming in. This continuous flow of work was their key. No matter what other projects did or did not happen for them, they felt they were safe with this larger client.

They knew about my general plan to start my own business soon, and the owner understood this desire as he too had once made the same choice. One day, he warned me about the ups and downs that come with starting this sort of business. Many people don't realize what goes on behind the scenes to make sure they have a job. That they themselves have had to go through a number of famines. Thankfully, one of the guys was able to reconnect with his old employer and start to funnel in a constant workload.

My employer had a similar setup with roughly 10 employees. They had 2-3 larger clients that were sourcing most of their income to employ us. I started noticing that these larger clients were giving my employer less and less work. It seemed like things were starting to dry up for them. Some of my coworkers and I found ourselves spending more time at sports bars with our boss than we were at meetings with clients. I knew this couldn't last much longer, so I decided I'd better have something else ready soon.

My plan was to save as much money as I could before the paychecks ceased coming in, and then go full speed with my own entity. This plan would need a few months before I was safe enough without any other income coming in. The work was drying up at my job, but it didn't seem like it would be a problem to last a few more months.

Then the first warning hit. One Friday morning after coming into work, the company's owner introduced us to an older man. Our boss was selling the company to a large software consultant agency. The merger was effective immediately, and we would all start reporting to work at the new office the following week.

Before the merger, our small team would meet with companies, figure out what a given company's needs were, and then hire the people to work in our office to complete the projects. This new company primarily was just a headhunter service. They communicated with companies who were looking for employees with particular skills and then found those types of people. The new employee would report to work at that actual company but be paid by this headhunting agency. Other than the paycheck, you were basically an employee of the company where you worked.

At first, this merger seemed like a gift. The new company didn't really know what to do with us. I wasn't a billable commodity that was put out on contracts for months at a time, and they didn't really want to give me a desk in their office. Only the recruiters had desks. Nobody in the software field worked at their very large office.

I would meet with the clients we were helping, but then I had nowhere to actually do the work. The client themselves didn't want me doing it at their office either. This was a golden opportunity for me and was the start of me working from home because I had no other option. I got to wake up and work on projects for my office job and then field any calls I may have coming in for my side projects. The only time I had to leave was if there were any scheduled meetings with the clients.

It was a glorious month or so, but it was too good to last much longer, and was only a matter of time before my office job figured out how to place me full-time somewhere. I had to take things in my stride as my own business was still in the building phase and take advantage of this freedom for as long as I could.

CHAPTER 5

Have a Backup Plan

I had a scheduled meeting one morning, so for once I had to actually get myself ready to head to a clients' office. The local news was on my television as I came in and out of my bedroom while I was getting ready. It was then that I saw the smoke coming from the first tower of the World Trade Center in New York. While standing there watching and listening to the news anchors discuss what could have caused this damage, I looked on with horror as a plane crashed into the second tower. Like most people, I couldn't believe my eyes.

I continued to watch for a while longer but then I started to wonder if I still now needed to actually go to this meeting or not. This client was a major cable provider and had a room full of TVs that they used to monitor all of the different channels at once. It was unclear still if I needed to go in, but I knew that they all would be in that room watching dozens of channels simultaneously all covering the unfolding situation. Being there in that room and seeing the constant coverage all at once on so many channels is still very much stuck in my mind. The world as we knew it would never be the same.

9/11 had changed everything. Many companies weren't willing to take the same level of risks as they did before. The economic slowdown thus accelerated. Most people and businesses were in a state of shock, and it certainly seemed like nobody wanted to focus too much on work.

Within only two weeks, rumors started swirling around about possible layoffs coming soon at my company. I guess the level of projects we had was not enough for this company to continue with us as their science project. The economic downturn had pushed this over the edge. This was combined with the fact that some of the clients didn't want to keep working with this much larger corporate company. I had heard from some of them that our price had gone through the roof once we were bought out. Regardless, I was hoping this layoff process would take a while. I was growing closer to getting enough projects of my own, but I needed this job to last a little longer. My fingers were crossed.

It seemed like at least one person was let go every week. My turn finally came on 10/3/2001. My last official date of employment with another company ever. My private layoff meeting with one of the owners still sits vividly in my mind. I don't think they knew I was planning on building my own business at the time.

I was given the usual colorful positive words about how good of a worker I was, and how I should have no problem finding work elsewhere. They were truly sorry that they had to let me go, but the economy was forcing them to do so. In other words, I was hearing the usual standard level of bullshit a company must give when they are firing someone. They even handed me a smaller final paycheck than I was owed because the client I was working with was angry that they let me go and I would be unable to complete the project. I might have been able to fight it, but that would only eat up much of my valuable time. I had to act fast to get my business running full steam now. The problem was that it was roughly 5-6 months earlier than I wanted to be on my own. I didn't have any major sustainable projects yet.

How could I possibly handle this? Most companies were laying people off. Trying to find a short-term job or even a job in general would be difficult. I fully believed that my experience and skill were good enough that I could find something. I contacted a few recruiters I met along the way, and they immediately began trying to place me in full-time positions.

The problem was, most of the time they didn't really bother to look at my resume. They would often try to connect me with positions relating to skills at the very end of my resume that I only spent a week or two using once a few years ago. Recruiters are notorious for using software that basically parses you into a huge keyword list. It takes away any emphasis you might have on your resume that highlights what technology you excel at.

To them, you are best at all of the words/skills found on your resume. They'd even find older companies who were still using outdated technologies I had worked with in my early years. Sure, I could handle these technologies again, but I didn't really want to get myself stuck using these so out of date now.

Beyond this, I knew that interview processes always took a lot of time. I may hear from the recruiter one week, and get a call from them the following week to set up a phone interview. If that went well, it may take up to a week for them to call the recruiter back. Then an in-person interview may take another week. Afterward, it may take them weeks to decide who to hire.

I lived on unemployment checks for a couple of months while I was looking at possible temporary office jobs. In the meantime, I was trying to find my first few larger clients. One of my now former company's clients was a part-time musician, and I would meet up with former coworkers at this client's performances late at night to vent our frustrations. This started getting me more and more into the local music scene, and reignited my interest in marketing services for clients in the music industry. This eventually opened up some opportunities for me. Now I had found a few small clients, and they related to an industry that excited me.

I hadn't found the right full-time office job yet, and these new projects would be under way within a month or so. Nothing serious was coming out of that process, and I could see that things would only get more unpredictable. Many of my friends had been laid off and some had already been laid off again in a matter of months from newer jobs.

The technology scene was suffering terribly in St. Louis. While the economy was still hurting everywhere, it seemed that the economies of the larger cities were able to fend off some of the heavier downturns. Because of this, I felt it was the right time to move back to Los Angeles. St. Louis was just not the right place for me to be trying to start a new business from scratch while the economy was suffering. Things seemed to be on an upswing there and I would be knee deep in these new projects in a short time.

About a week before I was about to move away, I got offered a large salary job that nearly made me change my mind. Finally, I had an offer that seemed promising, and it was right at my exact skill level. But I had already convinced myself to leave town. So, then, what was I to do? How important was money to me? Was it worth more than pursuing a feeling I had deep in my gut? No.

I finished packing everything into a storage unit and drove back to Los Angeles with my cat Ramses. I would return within a few months to get my stuff out of storage once I was settled somewhere. I drove as fast as possible and spent as little money as I could. I had saved as much cash as possible during my time as an employee, and now every dollar I spent was chipping into that. I knew I needed to get focused and fast. I even conducted a possible new client conference call from a hotel room.

Once I arrived back in sunny Southern California, I opted to rent someone's garage that they turned into a fully furnished month to month studio apartment near the California Institute of Technology in Pasadena. I wouldn't need to be there that long, I thought. I just had to get things rolling as soon as possible.

I settled in and started making phone calls to all of my various potential clients. What seemed like a good list of prospects over the last few weeks was suddenly falling apart rather fast. The main person at the larger of these new potential projects was killed in a car accident. Now the company would not move forward with any of their projects, and his partner was planning to take a full-time position at a company. That was the end of it. Another client I had previously been in communication with was now being bought out, so all of their previous plans were now canceled. One other client decided they needed extra time to get things ready. It would be several months before we would come back to discuss things.

Though I don't think they could've really helped me much at that time, this is when I learned a valuable lesson about the importance of contracts. I wasn't prepared for the floor to fall out from under me so fast. I should have had a backup plan.

CHAPTER 6

Wheel of Services

It became clear to me early on that while it was good to have billable clients, there would still be limitations on how much money I could make in a given week. This was something I learned from my office jobs. With each employee that was hired, they now had another person they could bill out for an hourly rate to a client. But with each of these new employees, the company needed to find more billable work to pay these people.

It is a never ending cycle and there will always be a ceiling to how many billable hours an employee can work each week. The only true way to have additional capital coming in was to build services that didn't rely on this per hour formula. Services that can run on their own with little assistance are often called passive incomes. You can utilize passive incomes to create a "wheel of services" that is pulling in income for you around the clock. One service by itself may not be enough to sustain you financially, but a series of them all available at the same time can add up to your desired daily income.

They say necessity is the mother of invention. If you are like me, business ideas will be flowing through your mind all day long. Most of mine never make it past the first few thoughts, but some will last a few days. Most of those will least get researched until I realize that they just aren't truly feasible or an acceptable profit margin may be in doubt.

An idea for a website had been in the back of my mind for a while. I went back and forth in my mind questioning why I would get myself involved in running something that meant constant supervision and customer service. This is probably the point at which panic sets in for most people who are close to launching their business, and then they'll suddenly stop their idea completely. They feel intimidated and then talk themselves out of it. They may think, "It will just fail. Why waste my time on something that I will lose money on?"

In the past, I didn't think I would have the time to be able to run a website like this. I was too busy trying to work my day job, start my consulting business, and plan a move back to another city.

The early days of me working on the chat service that also promoted musicians had left a lasting impression on me. I still had an interest in online marketing for musicians. I was already working on websites for musicians, and now I was in Los

Angeles—a hotbed for the film industry. From time to time, I would hear my musician clients talk about how they really wanted to license their music in films. Getting the attention of major film studios was very difficult though and rarely lucrative. Like many areas of the film industry, the people on top make most of the profits. Those at the bottom pick up the leftover scraps.

In my effort to expand my web client base, I had started attending film events to mingle with filmmakers. I wanted to help them with their websites and online marketing. I started noticing that these filmmakers were just as underfunded as the musicians I was already working with. All trying to make it big, but with very little money to spend on their own films. One comment I heard often was about how expensive it was for independent filmmakers to use a song by a well-known band. Everyone knew these songs, but it just wasn't possible for them to pay the crazy licensing fees.

As a web programmer, there had to be a way I could bring the two parties together: musicians and filmmakers. I wanted to help them, but every time I thought about taking the leap, I would back off. A well-known problem for artists is that they usually have very little money. Where would my own profit come from if these people had very little money? Plus, developing this website was going to take up lots of my time. Inside I had that urge to help solve a problem for them, but at the end of the day, putting food on the plate is always the most important thing.

Normally, I needed to be focusing on my clients so this idea wasn't being addressed. Here I was now, though, with not much of a client base. Finding new clients takes time, and a recently completed move had depleted most of my funds. Sitting and staring at the walls wasn't going to help me find money. My mind was racing. What was stopping me now from building out this idea? Now all I had was time and very little money.

One night I was watching and listening to some Opera on my local PBS station. Maybe it was the overly dramatic tone of the Opera, but my anger had reached it's peak. I had had enough of this situation. What did I have to lose, exactly? My back was against a wall. All the tools I needed were in my own hands and mind. So I started brewing a pot of coffee and began developing a website.

I was on a mission. Day and night began to merge together. Within 3 days, I had laid out the foundation for the site, a way to help independent filmmakers and musicians connect and work together. I described it to most people I knew as matchmaking for artists.

Within a few days of posting online to various groups and message boards, the memberships started trickling in. It felt amazing to build something from scratch that was helping people all over the world, and (of course) make myself money even while I slept. I had built myself my first passive income site.

It's not an easy concept to maintain. I had to constantly be advertising and marketing to both sides in order to keep it going.

My focus was more on the smaller film projects since it seemed no one at the larger film companies bothered to care about those. Sure it was quantity over quality, but it was something.

Some musicians hated it. Every so often I would receive hate mail about charging membership fees just to be able to look at film listings needing free music. Other musicians understood what I was going for. They knew that some of these projects were only door openers. It allowed them to meet other filmmakers and continue to find more work. With each successful project they could move up the pay scale or they could earn small amounts of pay for multiple projects all at once. Many of these films wanted to use already completed songs. This meant the musicians didn't necessarily need to do any additional work to their already completed songs. Just allow a filmmaker to use their song in a film and they could make additional money.

The service became a solid source of income for myself. It never took full control of my weekly schedule, but it certainly captured much of my attention over the next several years. I was often invited to speak at events about the film or music industry, as well as be involved in producing films myself. This site also helped me to locate additional web clients in the process. It definitely did its job. It made feel good to offer a much-needed service to an industry that desperately needed help and be able to make some extra money for myself in the process. In the end, that's the most we can hope for in a career.

So, with my first source of passive income to help back me up,

I felt a little more secure about myself. Now, I needed to find more clients. Thankfully, the potential client who I spoke with from my hotel room contacted me about working on some personal projects of his. After completing those, he then started asking me to work on projects for his corporate job. It seemed things were finally moving in the right direction.

CHAPTER 7

Morals and Money

There is a line for most people that they believe they would never cross over. It is when the chips are down that we sometimes have to rethink these boundaries, and then determine what is most important to us.

I now had one solid client, but I did not feel that I had enough guaranteed work to sustain me for too long. It was imperative that I got the assembly line of flowing. I needed to be working on a project while locking down a contract with another client, and fielding phone calls and emails with other potential clients - all at the same time. Project seeds needed to be planted, so that they would be ready by the time I was ready to start.

In the early 2000s, there just weren't that many places to look for online projects yet. You could try posting on a series of message boards or classified sites, pay for print magazine ads, hand out business cards at networking events, or set up booths at conventions.

Craigslist was by far the most popular website to look for goods and services in your local area. I even knew a few people who used it to find dates. It was known to be the Wild West version of the Internet since there were so many scams posted on the site. You couldn't fully trust what was available on it. Many of the dating postings were either fake or cover-ups for prostitution. The odds of finding a decent client on there were very low, but I couldn't be too picky. I needed more work.

Most job postings on Craigslist rarely mentioned paying you for your work. Offering no pay was usually an easy giveaway that it was probably a scam. These people all had such amazing ideas that they expected you to work for equity only. You and the job poster would be rich once you developed their amazing idea for them. What usually ended up happening, though, was you never hearing from them again after you finished their project.

Finally, one day I found a legitimate job posting that didn't seem to be half bad. It mentioned outright that they would pay for the work needed. They were a photography studio and wanted help with some web development. They needed something to help them maintain their galleries of photos from their shoots.

It was their hope that something dynamic could be written to help speed up their activities. A few emails were sent back and forth, and everything seemed fine so far. They just wanted me to come into their studio so we could finalize the details. So a meeting was set up for me to come into their office.

The first thing I noticed when I arrived outside their studio was how curiously discreet it was. There was no sign out front. This isn't really uncommon, though, in Los Angeles. Many businesses want to keep themselves away from the public eye. It makes it easier to work.

I buzzed at their front door and then waited for it to open. Upon entering their building, I went into their main office room and started hearing some strange sounds coming from the back of the room. It sounded like a woman moaning. I through a large glass window at the back of the room and could see into a large studio. There was a nude woman lounging on a couch. I was in a porn studio.

They needed me to enhance the membership section of their website. Every time they posted a new gallery of images, an employee would have to create a new set of HTML files to display all of the pictures. This meant hundreds of files were manually created and edited by someone, and that can be very time-consuming. Writing some code to do this automatically would save a massive amount of their time.

But this was for a company that many people would find to be dishonorable. How would I handle telling people about this client? Would it affect other clients' opinions of me? Would they not want to work with me because of who else I had worked with? These were all questions that went through my mind. It shouldn't matter who I worked with before. As long as I did their work, that's all that should matter.

They specialized in erotic photography, and as far as I could tell, nothing illegal was being done there. For me, that's the most important point. But if it's something legal, yet not something I am comfortable with, I would definitely pass on the project.

As software developers, we can be confronted by people from all walks of life. Who are we to tell others what they should and should not be doing? If it's a project for something that will make it hard for you to sleep at night, then certainly say no. What about my own morals? Sure, it wasn't a client I would proudly show off to everyone else, but I needed the money. I completed the work for them and continued looking for more clients. I believe I did one other small project for them, but then nothing else came out of this relationship. I continued networking and eventually grew busier elsewhere anyway.

This wasn't the only time I dabbled in the darker corners of the Internet. A guy I had met through my final office job from years back contacted me. He wanted to hire me to build a website with a membership area. Still desperate for projects, I quickly accepted. He had bought himself a high-end camera and was starting to do pornography photo shoots with several local ladies in his area. Members would be billed on a monthly basis and have access to these sets of photos. For me, the programmer, the code was no different than any other site I would develop that had a paid membership area.

He eventually hired me for a few more projects of his. His

mother had been a lifelong psychic and normally did most of her readings over the phone. Some of them were even conducted through a premium 1-900 pay-per-minute service. Apparently, she did pretty well as a psychic and at one point had even been on television for it. He wanted to set up a website for her that would allow people to purchase readings online. Whether I believed in this type of stuff or not, it was work for me. We continued to do some additional projects until his money ran dry.

Eventually, I worked on a breast implant class action lawsuit website for an attorney who had been referred to me. It was one of the simplest sites I ever built. It was mostly legalese with a few documents and submission forms. Strangely enough, I had more negative opinions from people about this site than I did about my past porn clients. Porn was shady but cool, yet these women who opted to get breast implants had "deserved" whatever ailment they received from their enhancements. Understanding the human mind is quite the task.

At this point, I still needed to find more solid clients. I needed consistent work—not these one-off types of clients. While porn notoriously gets a reputation for being easy money, I learned that this is not always true. I believe my friend never made much money from his sites. The professional studio I helped never really took off much either. I checked on their website years later, and it was still the very same outdated site I helped them with years before.

CHAPTER 8

Remember Your Supporters

A former coworker of mine had been referring me to a number of potential clients. He worked in sales at the web company that I had my final period of employment with. He lasted a few more months than I did so that he could help them land them a few more clients before they laid him off too. He was an easy-going person and just an all-around good guy.

As a non-local person to St. Louis, it was fascinating to me to see how he often he could walk into a bar somewhere and run into someone who knew him. He had such a laid back personality, and being a salesman appeared to come easy to him. If he had one possible flaw, it was that he wasn't very pushy. That may not always work with certain types of companies.

Even after I moved back out west, he and I stayed in touch. Eventually, he offered to help me find clients. Since it was already his job to hunt down Internet clients for his corporate job anyway, this wasn't too much extra work for him. Sometimes, people he would run into would need help, but maybe just not at the level that his corporate job offered. Many of these corporations only wanted the bigger projects that employed several people. I only focused on these smaller situations in my own business.

Most of the projects he found for me were great, but a few taught me some valuable lessons. I had recently started a project for a client he had sent me. Like always, I requested a deposit check before I would begin. Shortly before this, I had just created a new corporation in California and I was finally going to set up a new business bank account locally for it.

I used this new client's first payment as my first deposit while I was opening the new account. Two days later, their check had bounced. I was not only charged a fee for the bounced check, but the bank also charged me an overdraft fee as well. So my first transaction at this bank had left me in the negative until I transferred money over from my other bank.

I was furious. Here I was barely scraping by, just getting underway on my own, and this happens. I picked up the phone and immediately gave this client a call. They seemed extremely shocked that this had happened. Without any real incident, the client sent me a new check and included additional money to cover all the fees. This, of course, took a week to reach me. I had to ponder this situation while my new account sat negative until the check arrived.

Before I continue, I think it's worth mentioning that I sometimes hear people state that us independents with small businesses get stuck working with the bottom feeder clients. These are the clients with little capital and they are very prone to these sort of situations. I personally do not think that this is any better if you stick to only larger companies. They each have their own headaches. I've worked with a number of larger clients that were much worse about forgetting to pay or just blatantly delaying it as long as possible.

I've even overheard employees at larger corporations complaining about other larger corporations doing the same thing. No matter whether it is a large or small firm, companies and individuals will pull every trick in the book to wait as long as possible to pay out money. If your mobile phone company called you one day and said that you could wait one more month to pay your bill without any extra penalty, would you do it? Most people would. And they would wait until the final day to pay the updated bill.

This client did eventually connect me to a couple of other potential clients, but they all eventually disappeared from my active list. Thankfully, though, my salesman friend referred another client to me that worked out quite well. This client ran a local magazine and had a full in-office staff team. Their projects lead me to work with a wide range of technologies and they went on to be one of my longest active clients.

At times, I almost felt like a partner in their business. Sure I was paid for my time and effort, but it always felt like more. I was invited to multiple events of theirs and we had dinners together when they came into town. Ultimately they are just another client, but it's so much better when you connect in some way beyond the billable time.

Over time, my salesman friend and I fell out of close touch. He would contact me from time to time with possible clients and other ideas, but it's what he did in those early days that helped me during a very critical time in my career. We all have those stories about people who say they are going to help but never follow through. Everyone has their own life to focus on, but there are always people who make a difference in our life when we need it the most. What he did for me in those early days is something I will never forget.

A number of my clients have given me referrals over the years. Some have lead to better projects than others. I try to be fair to all referred clients, though none of the newer clients get any price discounts that the older clients received. A good portion of my current client roster all have come from referrals. Some were cold calls, but most were due to a trait I hang great importance on—making your clients happy. I make every effort so that they see me as more than just someone to complete their tasks. I try to create an on going dialog with all of them, and in some cases, we ended up becoming good friends.

CHAPTER 9

Handling the Unexpected

In 2005 I found myself splitting my time between being a web consultant and owner of an online film music placement website. I would work with my clients and write software during the day and then sit on music panels in the evening critiquing how people's music could be used in movies.

After a while, another idea came to me. Many of these musicians and filmmakers all needed help with raising money. This wasn't as popular of a concept as it is now. There were a few platforms available in 2005 to help people raise money, but nothing very robust. I decided to build an initial prototype website to see how it would work out and then hopefully seek grander funding of my own afterward.

At the same time, my client-turned-friend's company had decided to create a corporate health care enrollment website roughly 10 years before Obamacare (Affordable Care Act) existed. I was selected to handle this large project, and it is still probably the biggest project I ever took on by myself. Phone calls and e-mails were conducted about the basics for what needed to be done. His company felt that this was something that required a face-to-face meeting with me, something I don't do very often for non-local clients.

They offered to cover my airfare and hotel if I was willing to come in for the meeting. So, we scheduled a formal meeting to go over the entire plan. This meant I would actually need to get dressed up with a tie and everything! It would give me a chance to get out of the house, be paid for my entire trip, and see my friend in the process.

This project took place before many of the template-based technologies were available like they are now, and the most popular programming language was PHP. jQuery was only starting to become more widely used, and cloud services were still being more commonly called clustered networks. Building this product at that time was a much bigger challenge than it would be with the available technologies of today.

I spent many of my nights researching and planning the fine details and what questions I would ask at the meeting. For a small business like myself, a project like this could take up the majority of my time for the next few years. A wrong move could mean the difference between losing the project and myself missing out on a huge chunk of money.

I typically only hired designers or extra developers on an as-needed basis. This is always the hardest part of keeping things simple. You don't want to have the overhead of a full staff team. Trying to keep a network of partnered developers can be tough sometimes. Either they get too busy when you need them most or they eventually fall back into an office job and you never hear from them again.

I had had some limited success with outsourcing, but not too much. At the time this project was going on, it was much more difficult to locate a trustworthy outsourcing company to partner with. So I opted to start the project alone and wait until the situation called for something more. Only then would I sound the alarm and reach out to any reputable developer I had worked with in the past.

From the first moment we discussed the project, their biggest concern with me was that I was basically a one-man operation. They would voice their concerns and mention "what if" scenarios while on conference calls. They were scared that something might happen to me during the duration of this project. I was a young 20-something healthy guy, and I didn't really see why they should be worried about me. I rarely took much risks, wasn't currently playing any extreme sports, and at that time barely traveled outside of my city. I always dismissed their concerns quickly and the meetings would move on.

The craziest concern they would always mention was "What happens if you are hit by a truck? Who will take over the project?". I always laughed it off. How terribly negative of them to be thinking this way. "Nothing is going to happen to me", I would always tell them.

A friend of mine had contacted me one day before Memorial Day weekend to see if I wanted to have dinner. He didn't have a car, so I would have to drive down to his neighborhood. That evening, I picked him up and we left to go eat at a popular sushi restaurant. Afterward, we made for a small café about a mile away to have some coffee and possibly listen to live music.

The area this café is located in has some of the worst options for finding a parking space, so most people end up going a couple of extra blocks away to park near many of the neighborhood houses. After circling around for 10 minutes, I finally found a spot to parallel park on a quiet little street just 2 blocks away from the café. I had parked in this same area a number of times in the past when I had come to this same café.

I finished parking and then we both exited my car. As the passenger, he exited right out on the sidewalk. For me, the driver, I had to walk around my car to get to the sidewalk. Just as I began to make my way between the rear of my car and the car parked behind me, I heard a loud crash. A large black SUV had crashed into a truck about 2 cars behind me. This truck was then shoved forward into the car behind mine.

The force of this hit shoved the car forward just as I was walking between them. Seeing this all happen out of the corner of my eye, I did manage to attempt to jump and dive out of the way, but everything happened too fast. The car slammed into my rear bumper, and my left leg was still in between the two vehicles.

This impact broke my left leg and the rest of me was badly bruised. I could see the SUV and the driver to my left as I knelt there in pain with my left leg still stuck between the cars. The force of the impact was so hard that it stopped the SUV's engine and I could see steam blowing out of the radiator. He tried to restart the SUV and drive it away, but thankfully he only made it a block before the SUV's engine died again. People in the neighborhood, who had heard it happen, managed to surround him and make sure he didn't get away. I had been hit by a drunk driver and it wasn't even 7pm yet.

I was taken by ambulance to the nearest hospital, and my clothes were cut off me as they checked me over. I still remember the doctor being very surprised that I wasn't in worse shape. I only broke parts of my left leg. Nothing more serious than that thankfully, and I didn't end up needing any surgery either. I came home that night full of medications and a new Velcro cast around my leg.

The first thing that crossed my mind that next morning was about this project and the planned trip that had already been set up. I had to somehow still make this work. Canceling this trip would greatly damage my reputation with them. Unlike an office job, I couldn't take sick leave and delay the start of this project. As an independent, I don't get that luxury. When I say I will do something, I have to follow through on it.

I now had 6 weeks to be able to walk again and make this

flight for my meeting. What these people feared had basically happened to me, and I was afraid they might cancel everything. I needed to show up at the meetings and act completely normal. Many of these people had never met me, so they didn't have any prior history to judge me on. During the time I was in their office, I needed to be normal. This meant I needed to walk on two feet without needing a cane.

I would need to inspire myself to get well sooner than expected, so I started channeling the training montage scene from Rocky IV. I worked hard on my physical therapy and was able to walk slowly without a cane by the time the meetings were held. I hid my pain well enough during the meetings to not alarm them but I had to peel my sock off every night from my still very swollen leg and foot.

The first couple of months afterward were very challenging for me. I needed to stay focused but I was in near constant pain. Even now as I sit here writing this book, I still have pain from this incident. It has never fully left.

For reasons like this situation, I started creating a better network of supporting developers and engineers that I could fall back on if the time were to ever come again. I didn't want to be stuck in a situation like this again where I could not rely on some kind of backup. I was "lucky" in that only my leg was broken and not my arms or hands. I was able to work in my bed with a laptop, but would have been devastated without any working hands.

CHAPTER 10

All of Your Eggs in One Basket

Within a couple of months the project got underway, and it was more work all at once then I had ever done before. I considered opening a small office in a building near my home, but I kept stopping myself from overspending. I also considered hiring extra developers to help me, but the work flow was manageable as long as I worked at least 60 hours a week.

This usually meant eating dinner and then returning right back to work. Or it could also mean additional time on the weekends. I would do whatever it took to keep pace. I would think to myself, "Why share the money with anyone else if I could handle it?" Besides, I was still recovering from my injuries, so that kept me close to home anyway. Being stuck near my computer all the time made it very easy to constantly be working.

The client then gave me an extra incentive that if I could reach a particular milestone by a certain date about 1 month away, I would get a bonus payment. I billed on an hourly basis anyway, so whatever extra time I needed to put in to reach this milestone also meant extra money. I nearly gave every waking moment to this project, and I reached the goal without any real problem.

This project would continue on for nearly 2 years and my personal life nearly disappeared during that time. I almost completely stopped looking for any extra clients. All of my passive income projects and new ideas took a bit of backseat while I handled the busier aspects of this large project.

It wasn't easy for me to see at the time, but I had also mentally taken a hit from my injuries. I had actually been injured both physically and emotionally. Going through this traumatic event made me feel more vulnerable and mortal, and my willingness to take chances wavered.

I decided to table the fundraising site and just focus on this massive project, a few other smaller clients, and the film music site. My mind just couldn't take any additional distractions. It seemed that within a year or so after I tabled it, everyone was talking about Kickstarter. Would my site have competed? Who knows.

I wasn't entirely focused on it. I did not have employees to devote to it, but I may have at least been able to get a small piece of that market. I made my choice, though, and I can't change anything about it now. Ideas are always easy to come up with. How they are executed is what will make or break them. At the time, I simply did not have the motivation any longer to devote to this idea. I had become so focused on the health care site that not much else mattered anyway. It was consuming so much of my time and money was rolling in, what else could I ask for?

This project certainly seemed great for me at the time, but something terrible was lurking behind the scenes. I never bothered to hire anyone else full time to help with it so I could find other large clients. This project ate up the majority of my time every week as it was, while all other clients would come and go with only smaller requests. At the project's peak, I was working night and day 7 days a week to handle everything. I thought that eventually it would all slow down enough anyway, and hiring someone full-time would have been unnecessary. I was greedy and I wanted all of the money just for me. Being greedy is never a good thing.

Time continued to fly by and the calendar rolled into 2008. One day while out grocery shopping during lunch, I received a call from my friend at the company. They were being bought out by a much larger national insurance chain, and he wasn't sure what that meant for my project.

Like in most cases of this nature, the project manager told me that nothing was going to change. The new owners liked the idea for our site and wanted us to continue building it. Once the buyout was fully complete a few months later, though, I started noticing that my work load was dropping fast. Within only a few months after the announcement, my work load went from 90%

of my week to less than 10%.

I had been escalating my search for new clients and projects as fast as possible but I was having a harder time than normal finding new clients. The economy had started declining due to the bursting of the housing bubble and the subprime mortgage crisis. Fewer people now had money, and I was only able to find smaller sporadic clients. Panic was setting in.

Not only had I given all of my time to something that was never completed, but I had also devoted myself to only one form of technology. Software trends and methodology had been changing directions while I was deep in my project and I rarely paid attention to what technologies people were now talking about. I had so little extra time each week outside of this project that I had missed the warning signs. At the end of my day, all I was caring about was whether my clients were happy. I forgot the important lesson of always making sure to have one eye fixed on the prevailing trends.

As software developers, we need to be working on our latest projects but also spending extra time following what direction and methodology the trends are heading in. Corporations may be more reluctant to work with someone without any experience in new methods or technologies. I had dug myself into a hole during the worst time. The economy was bad and my own knowledge was becoming dated.

CHAPTER 11

Stay Healthy

When I first started working for myself, the concept of paying for my own health insurance was something I knew very little about. At my office jobs, I had medical coverage provided by the companies. Now, off on my own, it was something I had to consider in my budget every month.

It is now a requirement to have health insurance here in the USA. You will have to pay a penalty during tax season if you can't prove you had health insurance for the previous 12 months. This requirement is currently a hot topic around the US. Will this forced health coverage be reversed? Or will the system experience a massive overhaul? It's hard to say right now.

I have heard that many younger people are opting to pay the penalty rather than paying a monthly premium, even rejecting to sign up for those bare minimum plans the government is making available. They can afford to pay the penalty because it is much less than the long term prices for having annual coverage. But back in the early 2000s, this was not the case. You could go without any health insurance if you chose to. There were no penalties.

In my earlier years, I took a major risk by not having any insurance. I was around 22-years-old and still actively exercising most days. I had always been fairly athletic. Good enough to compete, and just slightly above average in my results. Ultimately, I at least knew that staying in shape kept me feeling energetic and my mind sharper.

I thought, "Why should I get health insurance? I was in my early 20's, felt good, and had no real health problems." I didn't have a lot of clients yet, and having to pay a monthly premium was something I couldn't afford. Yet in the USA, you are possibly eligible to write off your health insurance premiums as a business expense if you are self-employed. (Consult with your accountant fully on this.) If you can afford to have the insurance, it's money you can write off on your taxes and potentially help you to pay less during tax season. This is good in theory, but what if the price is just too much for you to afford every month when you need that money to cover other "more important" bills? Or even food! It's a monthly commitment that some months you just aren't sure you will be able to cover.

There was a walk-in health clinic not too far from my home, and I could pay a flat price if the need came up to go in for simple medications. It's a little shocking to think about now, but I ran my life like this in my younger days. I'm sure I am not alone. I was hiking multiple miles per day on rugged remote trails or jogging down a busy street next to cars speeding by. Working from home probably did lower my odds of getting injured in a car, so there was probably a give and take to these situations.

As work continued to improve, that little voice in the back of my mind was telling me that I needed to get health insurance. I discovered that it was more difficult than I thought to find a decently priced plan for just one person. I guess this is how corporations help the insurance industry. Corporations cover hundreds, if not thousands of employees all at once. So the insurance companies offer massive bulk coverage plans at cheaper rates than one guy like me could get on my own. The plans were either really high or cheap but covered only the most limited amount of items. Just wanting to at least be able to say I had some form of health insurance, I chose one of these cheaper plans.

At least it was something. I quickly discovered that it barely covered anything. Dental and vision expenses were nearly the same price as if I had no insurance at all. I knew that once my work picked up a little more, I needed to find something else.

It was during this time period that I began discussing this large project that itself dealt with the health insurance industry. Then not too longer after, I was seriously injured by the drunk driver. Over the next several months, I went time and again to see doctors and use expensive machines for X-rays, MRIs, and more. Much of these items were barely covered by the cheap insurance plan I had. Sure, eventually, I expected to receive an insurance settlement from the person who injured me. The reality for me, though, was that because my insurance was covering so little, much of the settlement money I expected to win would just go to pay off the medical bills I was collecting.

Some items like physical therapy were not covered by my insurance, so I had to pay out of my own pocket. I had a vague idea that insurance settlements were usually slow, but I had no idea that they were 5 years slow. All of the money I had to spend out of my own pocket would not come back to me for years. The price tag was all starting to add up. The money I wanted to use to grow my business was now going just to help me walk again.

If I had had a better insurance coverage during this time period, it's likely I would not have had to pay as much to the hospitals. I would have been able to keep more of the settlement money for myself afterward instead of paying what I owed to everyone for my medical care.

This situation happened to me in 2006 and my hospital visits ended by the start of 2007. The chain reaction from this on my business was massive. I wanted to get better coverage, but I needed to get myself back on track with my work. The larger project began eating much of my time, so I put off getting better insurance even longer. I stupidly allowed myself to get so focused on my work that everything else was taking a back seat.

For better or worse, this went on for the rest of year. Then, 2008 brought on a terrible downturn in the economy, killed off this project, and I was left with very little money coming in. Work was bleak enough that I even canceled the cheap health insurance plan and had no coverage for about 6 months. The plan wasn't covering much anyway and with the small clinic nearby I could just visit it if need be. I had to become extremely cautious with my own health.

I did eventually discover that one of the larger local hospital systems in my area - Kaiser Permanente - offered individual plans. They were reasonably priced and seemed to offer a good enough range of coverage levels for one person.

Knowing that self-employed people in the USA can possibly write off their health insurance premium, I would highly recommend that you make sure you have at least an acceptable level of coverage. Think of this money as just passing through you from profit to protection.

We can't fully know the unexpected, but we can at least better protect ourselves from any injuries and negative situations that we may encounter.

CHAPTER 12

On-again, Off-again Projects

Shortly after the start of the economic downturn in 2008, finding the right clients became more troublesome. Trying to adjust to this new economy and determine who was serious and who was a pretender became that much more difficult. I firmly believe that many of these clients were convinced that their financial situations were better off than reality suggested. Nest eggs were vanishing and clients were cutting every corner they could. Sometimes their investors were stable one day, yet broke the next. This typically would cause a domino effect all the way down to us lowly software engineers.

Considering that the point of a business is to make more than you are spending, I understand that it's nothing new for businesses to try and save every dollar they can. The methods by which this is achieved seems to get more creative the worse an economy gets.

Let's say a potential client contacts you with a new project.
After a brief discussion to see how legitimate it sounds, you sign
a Non-Disclosure Agreement. The client starts sending over lots
of details about the project. You then schedule a future meeting
to discuss what exactly they want to do. After another successful
phone call, money estimates are exchanged, and contract details
are discussed. Communication continues each day as they
continue to send you over additional project details about what
they would like for you to do. Things are really starting to build
up. You're beginning to plan your schedule around the work you
will soon need to do for them. The project is imminent.

A day passes and then two more. A full week then goes by
without a word. Not to seem too keen, you hold off from
contacting them. Another week passes and it's confusing you at
this point. Why would they go through this much effort and then
just vanish? You send them an e-mail. No response ever comes.

It's possible they found someone else, or maybe they just got
cold feet. Who really knows? Starting a business and taking
financial risks can frighten people. It takes lots of energy and
many times leads to failure. Sometimes people have a moment of
doubt right before crunch time and bail out.

Whatever their reason, it would certainly help to understand
what happened. It may be worth it to wait a month and try to
contact them again. E-mails are easy to be ignored. If you have a
phone number for them, people do seem to still answer those
though. Say that you were just calling to see if there was
anything you could do to help their business grow. Do take "No"

for an answer and let them be. This type of situation seemed to happen quite often during the economic slowdown, and it still occurs somewhat today. It's best to understand that it will happen to everyone and just move on.

Trusted clients are sometimes even guilty of this same behavior. They may schedule a meeting with you to go over a project and ask about your work availability for the short-term future. You go over the project, offer an estimate, and then nothing ever comes of it. It is possible they were just shopping around, and they wanted to see what you would charge compared to someone else. Depending on your relationship with this client, you may consider asking them point blank if they were shopping around. Sometimes just asking the right questions gives you enough clues as to what their agenda was.

I have learned to never give much attention to the potential of a new project starting, no matter what a client says. Until that deposit check hits my mailbox, or I am given the 100% *GO* from a retaining client, my mindset will not change. A project is just a potential source of income until it happens. I can not block out development time on a verbal statement.

Regardless of the client's actions, it's best to not get angry about this type of behavior, though. I try not to burn bridges at all costs. It's unprofessional and leaves a bad taste in my mouth. Unless you know for sure that you will never want to work with them or anyone they might know again, I would not do it.

I've had potential clients that took over 5 years for their first project with me to ever get started. I would receive details on a project, a quick call or two, and then no further communication. A year would go by, and then suddenly another e-mail would appear from them discussing the same project, only for them to vanish again not too long afterward. It's not worth more than making a phone call or two to try to push a project forward. Eventually, it either will happen or it won't, but don't waste much of your time wondering.

My advice is to say you are available for every single project that comes your way. As long as you expect to have the time available that is. What's the worst thing that happens? You are too full by the time that the project happens, and you have to tell someone "No". The flip side is that you tell someone "No" too early and end up missing out on a project when the original one fails to ever materialize.

CHAPTER 13

Traveling While Independent

Planning a trip some time soon? Know that many of your clients will come out of the woodwork with urgent requests the final days before you leave on your trip. So you better start preparing now.

And then always assume that the minute you leave for your destination something will more than likely go horribly wrong. For that matter, even assume something will happen while you are out running errands during a normal business day. Better yet, it's probably best to just never leave your house if you work independently.

All kidding aside, it's best to run through as many scenarios as you possibly can before you leave for any type of trip. In your head, run through as many situations as possible for each client. Think of anything that could go wrong or anything they may request from you while you are away. Have contingency plans for each of these scenarios. Have your laptop prepared with all software pre-installed so that you aren't using a spotty Wi-Fi signal somewhere just to download the software you need to work.

A few years ago, I had been planning a trip to Cambodia for several months. With only a month until I left, I had sent most of my clients a weekly reminder that I was leaving soon. I told them that there was a big chance that I wouldn't always have Internet access where I was going. Most of the clients weren't too worried, and they had no plans to bother me while I was gone.

Then with only a couple of days before I left, I was notified that during the time I was going to be away, one of my clients was planning to launch a massive website overhaul that we had been working on a month prior. They had been sitting on this completed project for over a month now and they had originally said it would be another month or two before they wanted to launch it. They had changed their mind and it would now be happening while I was gone. I tried to push them back with no success as they firmly believed there would be no issues. I held back my opinion. Something I shouldn't have done.

Everything that could go wrong with this launch did go wrong. The site launch wasn't implemented correctly, based upon my documentation to them, and they desperately needed me to help with it. All I brought with me on this trip was the most basic tiny Windows Netbook that took several minutes just to boot up.

My hotel Wi-Fi had stopped working about an hour before.

After getting additional information about the situation, I learned that the Internet was actually down across most of the entire city. I had to hop on the back of a scooter in the middle of the night and travel several miles further outside the city until we found somewhere with working Wi-Fi.

A restaurant we found was closed, but they left their Wi-Fi open all night long. I then sat on the side of a dirty dusty road in the dark with my laptop in order to fix the problem. In the middle of making some coding changes, the Netbook decided to force a software update that initiated the shutdown countdown. I then had to wait as the slow Netbook took its time rebooting again. It was a mess of a night for me, and I learned a valuable lesson. Or was it morning by then?

The timing of this launch was terrible. The trip was scheduled months in advance, and the site was not originally scheduled to launch while I was away. It was truly the perfect storm. I should have fought back harder about them launching it while I was traveling. My advice is to firmly persuade the client to wait until you are back to normal business. Explain that it's better to wait a week than to have a broken website.

It's better to warn all clients that no work will be done while you are away. Make them fully understand this. If a normal maintenance emergency occurs, always have someone you can trust who can help you in a pinch.

Sometimes you have very little control over certain situations. Several years ago, I had a hosting provider who decided to change a website's IP address without any notice. This client used the old fashion web server based e-mail relay software to send out all of their correspondences. The problem was that without notice their web server was switched to an IP that had previously been used by an abusive spammer. The IP address was still blacklisted by every major e-mail provider on the planet. None of this client's e-mails were getting to their people. The e-mails were either bouncing back or disappearing into the void.

My family was visiting from out of town and I had decided to take them sightseeing 2 hours away from my office. The client called and was extremely livid at me. They didn't quite get what was going on, but obviously in their own mind, it was something I should have been able to prevent. I wanted to break things. I was able to get the hosting provider to switch them to a safer IP address. Thankfully I was in wine country, and my wine couldn't be poured fast enough after the problem was solved.

I eventually moved this client from that hosting company, and was also able to finally talk them into using a third party e-mail relay service. It's great that services like Mailgun and Sendgrid exist today!

Not all of my travels have resulted in crazy stories. In fact, most of them haven't. I am happy that I can go anywhere I want, yet still have the option to be able to pick up my work if necessary.

Before I leave, I always thoroughly research my destinations and hotels to make sure that I have Internet access fairly readily. I attempt to limit the amount of time I am completely offline if there is any possibility of work issues creeping up.

Some international hotels do not offer Wi-Fi yet though. They still only have hard-wired Ethernet cables. This could be a problem if you are only bringing tablets or other devices without plugs for the Ethernet cables. You'll need to bring adapters of some kind to get connected to the cabled Internet.

My tool of choice is a travel router/external battery that fits in your hand and emits a Wi-Fi signal. This device plugs into the hard-wired Ethernet cables, and then transmits a Wi-Fi signal that you can connect all of your devices to. You can even setup a private secured Wi-Fi channel. Since it is also a battery charger it powers itself so you don't have to sit it right next to an outlet. It can be wherever the Ethernet plug is. You do eventually need to charge it, but they can last for most of the day without being charged.

As independents, we have the freedom to roam. If you are too afraid to break away for fear of losing clients, then you need to re-evaluate your relationships with them. We all deserve a little time off, and the best clients know that you will work better with a little time away.

CHAPTER 14

Reinvent Yourself or Become Obsolete

As the economy slowly improved, the popularity of software languages shifted every year or so. If I wanted to stay relevant, I had to always be evolving.

I had started in the tech field as a dial-up Internet reseller. Eventually, I was promoted to the company's Network Operations department configuring and maintaining the routers that ran the dial-up modems. From there, it seems I sped things up by evolving every couple of years between front and back end software technologies. Perl became uncool, so I moved to PHP. Python became popular for about a minute in the late 90s, so I then had to learn that too. JavaScript then wasn't good enough—everything became about jQuery.

It then became all about front end frameworks, no one was supposed to write vanilla code anymore. PHP went from being the language of choice, to the one many people ridiculed. Buzz picked up around Rails and then Python circled back around again with its own frameworks (like Flask and Django). JavaScript went from being just for the front end to being the basis for Node.js and Angular. I had to keep up with these progressions all the while learning and building mobile apps for Apple and Android devices.

I definitely left out quite a few steps along the way, but just writing the section above feels maddening. I guess every job has some level of continuous training to stay up to date, but my bias makes me feel like software development takes the top prize.

These days, everything has become more modular with packages and plugins rather than how much code you can actually write. If you are up-to-date with the ones everyone is using that week, you may very well still be a valuable programmer. OK, I am joking somewhat. It's tough to actually be working on projects as well as spending most of your extra time monitoring what's currently popular. Maybe for some die-hard programmers studying new languages is their hobby. For me, I prefer other interests.

In my opinion, I don't think it is worth the time or energy to constantly attempt to be on the forefront of what is trending in software. Why? I've seen too many of the hot-now-gone-tomorrow technologies. The tech industry reinvents itself so fast these days. If all I ever did was try to be "on the cutting edge", I feel I'd never actually do any real work. We must pick and choose wisely. Devote too much time to the wrong technology and you're obsolete. You only have so much time on this planet.

Unless you like riding the wave. Then go right ahead. You clearly have more time than I do.

Lately, I have been seeing more discussions about how most of the major Silicon Valley companies won't hire programmers over 40. People have to hide their age during interviews by wearing trendier clothes and hairstyles. At the rate this is going, I bet that age will drop to 30 in a few more years. Kids continue to learn how to program younger and younger, so why shouldn't that age shift ever further down?

So exactly why won't they hire older programmers? Older programmers can possibly be more set in their ways as far as what programming languages they want to use to solve a task. It's possible also that the methods and algorithms that younger programmers are being taught are entirely different and faster than those taught to the older generations.

Similar to how younger children now all learn an entirely different approach to how they solve math using the Common Core standards. Parents have an extremely hard time helping their own children with their math problems because the parents are entirely lost with this new approach.

What I've been lead to believe, though, is that children who learn math through Common Core are mentally able to crunch much larger numbers faster than kids of the same age who were taught the older methods. So while initially it's tougher to grasp, the long-term effect is much more positive.

If I use this same concept, it's highly possible that younger programmers may have a better grasp of certain technologies. Then there is the usual assumption that younger programmers have more energy, are willing to work longer hours, and are possibly more malleable in terms of absorbing new information.

As one of those older programmer guys, I will hold fast to my experience level. I've witnessed many different scenarios in code with many situations, and I feel I have a fuller idea of all the possible ways a situation could unfold inside the code. But I also know that age is going to fully catch up to me one day and I need to have other skills. Sure, I can be a project manager, architect, team lead, CTO, etc. I already do most of those now depending on the day of the week. But what about something non-technology related? Wouldn't it be a good idea to expand yourself outside of this field?

My solution to this was to try and become a more global-minded person. I opted to devote my extra time into learning another type of language. I decided to learn Mandarin Chinese. These days, I enjoy dropping myself into a different Chinese city every so often and, then immerse myself in the language for weeks at a time. It's scary as hell but very rewarding.

I'm not exactly sure how I will use my new language skills. It could lead to another career or it may be just for fun. All I know is that I won't always be able to compete with others as a software programmer. Kids just keep getting sharper at a younger age, and I can't seem to stop aging. By focusing my extra time outside of the technology field, I am utilizing one of my own lessons by not putting all of my eggs in one basket.

CHAPTER 15

Lost Wages

It is said that you have to spend money to make money. But what about money that you never actually made? Money that you could have potentially earned if you had stuck with your office job since they are often times more guaranteed as long as you aren't fired. Exactly how much more money would you have earned if you had stuck with your job?

A guaranteed salary can be nice, but they often have their ceilings. You know the max amount you will earn regardless of how hard you work. Sure, some companies offer stock or profit-sharing, but the odds of those making you filthy rich are low.

Most startups fail, and most solid corporations' stocks increase at a very slow and steady rate. This can certainly help your nest egg for retirement, but it will not make you rich now. There's always a chance for a promotion, but even that has its ceiling. Try to work on a side project while employed at a large company, and they may come after the rights to your project. They want to own all work you do while you are employed by them, so you'd better double check the agreements you signed when you first started your job. One thing is for certain, you will work long hours at your office job and may never see more than your set salary.

As you have seen so far in this book, working for yourself can be extremely risky and difficult. You can go broke by taking this path. But working for yourself can leave the door open for you to have as many side projects as you feel you have the time for. One lucky break with any of them and suddenly you are making twice as much as you did from your last office job.

This isn't something that happens immediately, and as I've previously mentioned freelancing can be a feast or famine of work. When it's in the famine mode, you sit at home with no work coming in, and no money in your bank account. You start to think about all of the money you at least would have earned if you had stayed with your office job.

The money that you could have been making during this famine is what many people like to call "lost wages". Money that you never actually received, but you could have earned if you had made a different choice.

Determining the exact amount of lost wages is a little hard to do. Stay the course, keep your office job, and you know where you will stand every week. Leave the job, start your own business, sit at home, cross your fingers that a major project finally happens, and have no real idea how much money you will end up making.

Some people start working for themselves because they think they will make more money than they did working for someone else. Others do it for the personal freedom.

Down times, also known as dry spells, happen often for independents, so the potential for lost wages is very high. At a 9am–5pm salary job, no matter how little work has been given to you, you will make a set amount of money each week. Yes, I completely understand that most 9am-5pm jobs now require much longer hours than that. Some people are working 60+ hours per week on a salary. Regardless of the actual hours you have to work, the fact is, you still are guaranteed your salary.

As an independent, if you have not locked down any work that week, you will not make any money. You will have plenty of time to sit at your house, read a book, paint, crochet, walk the dog, or even take a hike.

Sounds nice and relaxing. Until the bills start to roll in. Panic and anxiety become your business partners. Then you rush and take any project you can get your hands on for less money than you normally would, because something is better than nothing, right? Now you're working heavily on a project for less money than your office job. Even worse, now you do not have the time to seek out work for the payment rate you actually deserve. It's a double whammy.

Be very honest with yourself, why exactly do you want to work for yourself? If it's for money, then you have to be sure that you will make more than you would at an office job that you gave up. If it's for the freedom, then don't let your own business hold you back more than that office job would. Most average salary office jobs in the United States limit you to 2 weeks of vacation per year. Some have expanded this to 3 or 4 weeks.

The problem with many office-based software engineer jobs these days is that the competition has become extremely fierce. The rush speed that many of their projects need to be completed at does not allow many people to actually take their days off. Some employees are afraid to leave their job for too long, or they may not even have a job when they get back. The fact that you left at all shows that your job is not important enough for you.

As an independent, you have the ability to turn down projects if you have already set up vacation days. This can certainly cause problems too, but it's your choice whether you will let this control your life. I did once have a client who would come and go over the course of 3 years. We would sometimes go months at a time between communications; it had become a fairly common routine.

I once received an e-mail from this client asking if I could start on a new project for them the following week. Problem was, I had just landed in Beijing, China and would not be back home for another 2 weeks. I let them know the situation and asked if they could wait this 2 weeks for me to get home. I never heard from them again.

So, we too can lose out if we are not always available. It bothered me a little early on, but eventually I let it go. I can't run my life based upon someone else's time line if they aren't willing to compromise with me. Especially if it wasn't for something I had previously made myself available for.

CHAPTER 16

Social Animals

Paraphrasing an oft-mangled quote credited to Woody Allen, "80 percent of success in life is showing up". The accuracy of the percentage in this quote could be debated for hours. There is certainly much more that goes into success than just being in the right place at the right time. But I do believe there is some truth to this statement. It's hard to get noticed if no one ever sees you. Whether this is in the physical sense or through marketing yourself online, being invisible won't help you land clients.

I did land a number of my clients from just attending events and talking to the right people. Once while attending a music event here in Los Angeles, a popular speaker on stage spotted me in the audience and pointed me out to the crowd as a good recommendation for the marketing topic he was discussing.

Everyone sitting around me immediately was tapping me to

get my business card. I had only introduced myself to this speaker a few minutes before he went on stage. He knew of me and my company beforehand, but we had never met in person. Having someone give me social proof in front of an audience of three hundred was amazing. He had propelled me from an unknown in the audience to someone who had a hard time getting to the bathroom after the event was over. A line formed around me to get a chance to speak with me.

Some of the clients I connected with that day went on to refer me to other people and so on. This entire chain of events would have never happened if I hadn't gone that day. Once I was there, I didn't just stand in the corners. I introduced myself to a number of people. One who just happened to be a key speaker for the day.

I was fairly shy when I was young, and I rarely spoke up for myself. I always took the back seat and let others have all of the attention. I hated to be under the spotlight and had a hard time speaking in front of the class for anything. I would get sweaty palms, the nervous shakes, and would become disoriented. I was very timid, yet I was an athlete at the same time.

What I didn't realize back then was that my own mind was learning how to trick myself out of these terrible patterns. Deep down, I knew that I would always fail unless I broke out of this way of thinking. My mind was causing myself grief. So it seemed like an out of body reaction when I started raising my hand to go first for most speaking situations in the front of my classes. I was forcing myself to perform my task before my mind had a chance to destroy me. I had figured that out about myself. If I let my mind wander too far, I was a nervous wreck.

My confidence slowly started to come into its own once I moved away and had real work. While having personal conversations was still very hard for me, talking about software and technologies was much easier for me. It became easier to speak in a meeting in front of the company president and a number of staff members about technology, but I would go blank if I were to mingle at an office function.

This was going to be a problem for someone who was now self-employed and needed to attend mixers to network with potential clients. Attending these types of events is a must if you plan to gain a number of local clients. You can certainly gain one or two by cold calling and possibly even get a few other referrals. But that will take lots of time. It's true that mixers tend to be heavy on the booze and light on the meaningful connections. You are almost guaranteed to not get anything out of a mixer except maybe a hangover, though, if you just stand next to the wall all night and not talk to anyone.

If talking to other humans is something that scares you, then social interaction is a big challenge for you. If you have no interest in speaking with other humans and wish to remain in your home as much as possible, freelancing will most likely be even more difficult. I'm sure some people have mastered getting clients with very little social interaction, but I'm not one of them.

For those wanting to break out of your shell, just not convinced you can, let me give you a little advice. I was once like you. I know myself enough to know that if I quit attending these types of events for a while, I tend to recede somewhat back into my introverted ways. The first time I get back out there, I will feel somewhat lost.

First off, you should remember that we're all humans. Some people hide their flaws better than others. Most people who attend mixers are in "game mode", and have their sales face turned on. Some are even merely playing up a persona for the social atmosphere. I recommend you do the same. Create a different persona of yourself. Become an actor.

What type of person would you be if you could pull yourself out of your shell? Most of these people have no idea who you are, and you have a clean slate with them. Act as if you are this make-believe person temporarily. Focus on some other hobby or topic that interests you. That way, these people have something easy to connect you with. Are you that guy who always wears cat ties to the events? Be that same guy at every event. Sometimes, all we need is to "fake it, until we make it". First, we are faking that we are social animals. Then one day, suddenly we are that person.

Before you head out for the event, mentally prepare yourself for the evening. See the evening as a mission and set a goal for yourself. Say that you will at least walk up to a certain number of people that evening and have small talk. Start off small, even if it's only three people. Then go to your event, talk to your three people, and then head home if you want. Just saying "Hi" and walking away does not count.

Be the one who is asking most the questions, and let the other person talk the most. Since you are a little shy still, it will be easier for them to be the one talking. Walk up to someone, say hello, and then introduce yourself. Stick to simple topics, and bring up something basic about them. Are they wearing a piece of clothing that you like? Are they drinking the same beer as you? And then ask them about their work. What do they do?

Sometimes that's all it will take to land new clients. It doesn't have to be about anything important. Nobody wants to get into deep discussions while they are socializing at these events anyway. So what else should your small talk be about? If there is a speaker at your event, wait until the speaker has finished. After everyone returns to their normal socializing, approach someone who seems inviting and ask them what they thought about the speaker or the topic just covered. It's an easy lead in to start off the conversation with. You don't have to come up with anything else.

In my opinion, the most important skill you should have for every event is to be able to remember people's faces so that you can remember details about them. This is especially beneficial for remembering small details about them. Chances are they won't remember your name. Be honest, most people's names pass through one ear and out of the other before they even finish telling it to you. Understand that it's probably going to be the same for them remembering your name.

This is why it's important to at least remember their face. For me, that is much easier. I can connect a face with a detail they told me at a previous event. Don't just blurt out a detail you remember about them from before. Use it in a question. Ask them how that particular thing is progressing. You can see their face light up when you remember something about them.

Nowadays, I enjoy speaking at events. I still do get the jitters before an event begins, but once I hit the stage I find that the energy from the jitters quickly get transferred into a feeling of excitement for being able to speak in front of an audience. I now truly enjoy talking in public about subjects that matter to me.

So how exactly can you break out of your shell? I can't really speak for you. We are all different. It's like trying to figure out how to hack yourself. Trick your mind into working for you, since you know yourself better than others. Learn what things cause the biggest anxiety for you. Find confidence from other topics that do give you confidence. Attend events that cover those topics. Use the same goal of speaking to people at those types of events.

Once you feel that you have mastered your confidence there, transfer this same feeling you get into situations you aren't as confident. Be completely honest with yourself that you will either have to confront your public anxieties or accept that you may never be able to reach your business goals.

Tech-savvy people have it much easier to utilize the Internet to connect with people from around the world. If you can break out of your shell, you have the ability to create Youtube videos of yourself talking about your favorite technologies and topics. This gets you an even wider audience that you may never have reached before and can possibly land you additional clients.

Being more outgoing also allows you to create videos for sites like Udemy, where you charge people who want to watch your pre-recorded video lessons. By being less camera shy, you have now created an additional passive income for yourself. Some people are even brave and organized enough to teach public courses at places like The Learning Annex. Not only does this generate additional income for you, but it gets you additional validation from a fresh set of eyes. You never know who else they can connect you with.

CHAPTER 17

Work Smarter, Not Harder

I am lucky to have the abilities of a software programmer. Even my wife, who is a clinical lab microbiologist, has stated to me before that she wishes she knew how to write code. I'd be lucky to understand a tenth of what she does on a daily basis, but I always thank her for the compliment.

"Internet of Things" is now a thing. So many day-to-day activities are now being automated. Want your coffee ready by the time you get home? Use an app. Temperature not right at your house? Change it while still at work. It seems that a new company with a new device hits the market every month right now.

Plus, since the launch of the credit card sized boards like the "Raspberry Pi", it's become easy for the "makers" of the world to create whatever type of home automation suits their fancy. It will only be a matter of time until you have your own private robot at home. And then the robot revolution and uprising may be right behind that, right?

Today as a small business owner, wouldn't it be great to have some helping hands for free? Virtual assistants can certainly do the trick, but they cost money. As a programmer, we can help ourselves do daily mundane tasks just by writing some code.

Many of the computer languages can run your automated tasks. What language you use is really up to what you are comfortable with. I am not a snob when it comes to free labor. I mainly use Python, PHP for some older tasks, and a little PhantomJS.

I realized I was doing too much of the grunt work myself for a number of my tasks. I may only be one person, but if I truly harness my software skills, I can write programs to act as my evil henchman doing all the little dirty tasks that need to be done.

This even includes searching the Internet for new clients. By writing a good scraping program, I can have it scour the Internet for jobs that match my current programming interests. This includes job boards, Reddit, Craigslist, Twitter, Facebook, and more. I can have it search them all, and even rank the results in order of possible opportunity. I imagine that now I have well over 50 bot programs (or apps as the cool kids call them now) running for me all day every day.

Ten years ago, I only had a few running for me, but now that number has skyrocketed. This number increases fairly often, as something new crosses my mind that I could automate. These tasks include monitoring news headlines, scouring job boards for new projects that match my interests, finding chunks of code I need to learn about, letting me know when trends change, acting as salesmen and marketers, monitoring some foreign business trends in other languages, and many more tasks too tedious to mention here.

I'm glad children are learning to code at such early ages now. Knowing code and using Linux (my personal choice) is a game changer to me. I couldn't imagine my life without my bots and a handful of Raspberry Pis mini computers.

It's difficult to be constantly scouring for new clients while you are currently working long hours on projects. Using my bots to scan for other work is one way that has made it easier for me. Obviously, you could hire someone or an organization to be your salesperson and cold call for you. That can get expensive fairly quickly, though.

Some freelance engineers have tried to offer commission-based sales jobs to people, yet I think this rarely works out. Working in sales is already hard enough, but working as a commission-based headhunter for small freelance engineers will hardly make someone enough money to survive.

This is why some people have created membership-based services that can e-mail you job leads on a monthly basis. These companies are supposed to communicate with companies looking to hire and then e-mail out the details of what these specific companies need. Their e-mails go out to every paid member. Then it becomes a numbers game. How can you make yourself stand out from the rest of the people also responding to these same postings?

There are also a number of larger job websites that offer similar e-mails, but these e-mails are sent out to everyone who has signed up to their lists. They do not have membership fees, so this means you will be playing an even larger numbers game. This makes your odds even worse. How can you stand out against potentially hundreds or thousands of applicants?

From my own experience, it is best to craft one e-mail template focusing on your best skill. Hype up this skill, while only briefly mentioning that you cover other technologies. If you must, consider your second and third best skills. Also, craft e-mail templates that hype each of those skills up individually. If job opportunities come in for one of them, use that specific template. Leave room in your template for a personalized sentence about this specific job. When I say template, I mean a paragraph or two maximum. Everyone's time is valuable and most people's attention spans are extremely short. Make what little they see about you count.

I also use services like Talkwalker and Google Alerts to constantly be alerting me if new postings appear online that match my skills. These services are constantly monitoring the Internet for new web pages and postings. Anyone subscribed (it's free) to receive e-mails about a particular keyword will get notified. IFTTT and Zapier both offer something similar with all of their applets. You create an applet for a particular service (like Craigslist), and it will e-mail you immediately if something new is posted on that site that contains your keyword(s).

Whatever industry you work in, there has to be ways to automate some of the more mundane tasks you do every week. The examples I used above can all be utilized for whatever industry you work in. Brainstorm and seek out solutions to make your life easier. This way you can focus more on the things that make you money.

CHAPTER 18

The Pareto Principle

Over time, I finally felt like I had a good system in place for my company. Bots were handling my little tasks, I had a list of stable yet rotating clients, I was no longer afraid to network in public, and several supplementing passive income projects were helping me to pay my bottom line. I knew that I never wanted to let my guard down again, though, as there's always a way for things to go terribly wrong when you least expect it. To stop this, I knew I must be ready. I had to have backup plans for my backup plans. What I needed was a good formula to hold it all together.

Some of you may be familiar with the 80/20 rule. If not, here is the definition from Wikipedia: "The Pareto principle states that, for many events, roughly 80% of the effects come from 20% of the causes." I often try to see this theory in all things both good or bad throughout my daily life.

How does this relate to being an independent consultant? Here's an example formula I try to maintain in my business world. In general, 80% of the work I do comes from 20% of my clients at any given time. I try to keep this routine fluid and schedule clients accordingly. By leaving 20% work space open every week, this allows the other 80% of my clients not currently on my active project list to come to me with smaller requests.

This especially comes in handy for those clients that are basically just in maintenance mode. These are clients that I do not have an active project with. Maybe I did some work for them at one time, but now the project is live and the client is making money. But then they want a quick change or an additional feature they would like to have as soon as possible. By leaving 20% of my schedule open for them, I have the ability to handle their needs.

The good news is that if it is an urgent request, I get to look good for being able to handle it promptly. Plus, if I have my contract rates in proper order, I can bill that 20% space at a higher rate for urgent issues. This 20% opening is now making me income at a level closer to 40% of my work week.

If their requests will consume more than what I perceive to be 20% of my available time, I let them know that their request will need to wait. Once another project ends, the new request is added to my weekly rotation.

If you don't try to live by the 80/20 rule you may end up giving an equal amount of time to everyone and never get anything fully accomplished on time. Trying to multi-task too many things at once can wear you out fast. Plus, who wants to have eight bosses yelling in your ear all at once?

Another area I often relate this principle to is when it comes to new clients and projects. Trying to land new projects can be demoralizing to some. You spend lots of time and energy putting proposals together, talking on the phone, and sending e-mails back and forth. Then hopefully you land the project, but most of the time this doesn't work out. A potential client can simply vanish for many reasons.

Overall, I believe that roughly 80% of the projects that I have ever worked on came from only 20% of the people who have contacted me. That means that 80% of the potential clients that have ever come to me, I did not get. That's a huge number of people. I'm positive there are books out there who prove that I could have landed many more of these projects if I had persuaded them a little harder. I'm confident that this wouldn't have budged these situations much, though. That's how much I believe in these numbers.

I used to get saddened by the thought of losing that many potential clients, but over time I stopped letting it bother me. Everyone shops around and sometimes projects just vanish. You can't control outside forces like this, and there are so many possible reasons that a potential client went somewhere else.

The 80/20 rule often even applies to repeat clients. It wouldn't be too far-fetched to say that 80% of the repeat clients

I have had were 20% of those I have ever worked with.

As a programmer, I look at numbers, patterns, and code all day long. I'm often writing equations and statements that cater to finding these types of situations, so I guess it is only right that I see patterns in the day to day life I lead. My point is to find patterns in your work schedule and fine tune them until it works for you. Maybe it's a 70/30 rule for you. I just like the idea of leaving my door open a little for the "what ifs" of the work week.

CHAPTER 19

The Numbers Game

Every day it seems that there is more discussion about many of us losing our jobs to robots. Since I was a little boy, the concept of a robot has grabbed my attention. I know I am not alone since robots have been popping up in movies for nearly 100 years now.

So many of our devices at home are now "smart". We can easily have a robot make us a cup of coffee while we are driving home from work with just the tap of a finger on an app. Yet, companies like Starbucks still pull in massive amounts of cash on an annual basis from people coming into their locations. Those people working at your neighborhood Starbucks could also someday be replaced by a robot. Robots will eventually replace many of us at our current jobs. There's absolutely nothing we can do to stop this progression.

It's simply about how you perceive a situation. Many careers from 100 years ago are now gone. Plenty of them were replaced by factory robots. Is everyone now unemployed because of this? No. Humans adapted. New jobs were created from those situations. When one rock is overturned, another layer of opportunity arises.

The "Theory of Abundance" is the next theory I want to bring up. To summarize it, this is the belief that no matter how limited a situation may seem, there is always plenty of other options out there. This is the ultimate numbers game, so keep a positive attitude and focus on these options.

Lots of career websites will list software engineer as one of the top paths to consider. From my own experience, this is true. But the competition is fierce, and it is only getting tougher. Every year more and more people are learning to write code. Combine this with the fact that every year more children are being taught to write code at a young age. Then include the fact that clients also have the option to offshore their projects at a fraction of what you could possibly charge here in the USA. Combine all of these facts together and it can be a scary thought for someone who works independently.

So what does this mean for someone like me here in the USA? Time is not on my side. I am growing older every day. My biological hardware is slowly wearing out. I didn't learn to write code at the age of 5. I started at 17. I also live in one of the more expensive cities in the US. I can't possibly compete with the price of someone in Bangladesh.

A possible reaction would be to drop your rate in order to compete with these cheaper competitors. My own response was to actually raise my per hour rate. Why? Because I understood it and accepted the situation. There really is no way I could compete against an offshore developer. Why bother hurting myself even more by lowering my rate. I doubt it will do much to persuade someone.

Something strange happens when you charge a higher price. You've now limited yourself to a wealthier level of clientèle, and your options will be much fewer than before. The people who are willing to pay these prices perceive that they are getting something of higher quality. You must obviously be able to back up this belief. They tend to also believe you are a more experienced expert than someone who charges much less. Whether you are or not is entirely debatable.

I've often heard that competition is a good thing. Embrace your competition and accept that you can not compete against those who are willing to work for less. You should not let this be a detriment to your own career. Understand that sometimes people are willingly paying for what they get. Be able to see that clients who are willing to pay a higher rate often hold a higher standard in their own operation and expect the same from you. From my own experience, many of my best clients were the ones who were willing to pay me the most.

The "Theory of Abundance" basically tells you that you have plenty of options out there, so you should not cut yourself short. Be willing to say no to a client if they want you to work for less.

Let them see that you have other options. Sometimes this fact alone, gets them to understand you better and will shift their opinion in your favor. Never apply to projects offering to pay you less than what you normally want just because you are having a work famine. Be mindful of the changing industries and always be adapting. New ideas are created constantly, the Internet is expanding every day, and the world is always evolving. So evolve with it.

There are plenty of opportunities for you to find quality clients. Have you learned a new trending technology lately? If not, find the time. Open a new door to a whole new set of clients. Don't trap yourself into working on something for less money and miss out on noticing a higher paying project that passes you by.

I've always told people that I would much rather work less at a higher rate and have more free time to find additional projects, than always being too overworked and underpaid to know what day of the week it is. I've been there in my younger days and I won't go back.

CHAPTER 20

Will I Ever Get Paid?

Most typical salary jobs that you work 9am to 5pm (or later) five days a week in the United States pay their employees on a two-week cycle.

For us consultants, our next payment may come in a week or it might come 3 months from now. It's sometimes hard to know for sure. A project that looks like it will end in a few days may get put on hold for a few more weeks (or even months) as the client has an epiphany and wants to make additional changes.

Sometimes, right before the launch, reality hits the client. They will need to spend extra time and attention on their online business after the site launch. This sends them into a panic and they simply get too overwhelmed. So they decide to put the launch on hold for an extra period of time until they are ready to handle a new influx of customers. This can be anywhere from weeks to months, depending on how busy they are, and the time of the year. If you set your contracts properly, these additional changes will mean more money for you, but it also now means the project will close out much later than you anticipated.

I prefer all of my projects have an initial deposit. At least this way I have some money already in my bank account. My comfort level on the deposit amount differs depending on the prior history with the client. If you only ask for a deposit up front and then the remainder at the end of the project, I would highly recommend that you put clauses in your contract about project delays. Something that guarantees you a certain percent amount of money by a certain date, regardless if the project is launched or not. This way you are not just stuck with the initial deposit until the project finally launches; whenever that may be.

The best answer is to invoice clients every week or two, no matter what the status of the project is. You could give them a general estimate at the start of the project, but state that invoices will come every 2 weeks or month. Now you are not on their schedule anymore. Some clients may not like this idea, especially if the work is all being done on your own secured web server. They don't have access to the code, and they are giving you money for something they have only been able to demo. This can be a concern to them.

This is why some people go with the milestone approach. You can first ask for a deposit up front and then start cutting your work into chunks of tasks. After you complete each chunk of tasks, you can demo the work with them on your own server. After they agree (hopefully) with what you have done, you can move over everything you've done up until this point to a server or repository of their choice. You then continue your work on your own server until the next milestone is hit and a demo is completed.

Another reason you will possibly go without pay for an extended period of time is due to general "forgetfulness" *by the client*. Sometimes it is the truth, but from my own experience, the majority of the time it is just an excuse. For example, say a client tells you that they mailed your payment. This triggers you to start watching your mailbox day after day. Suddenly, a week has gone by. Either it was lost, they never actually sent it, or the old Pony Express was hired to deliver it by horse. Which of these do you think it is most often?

I once read about one of the best tactics business owners should follow. Unfortunately, I am not able to remember where exactly I heard about it though. The general idea is that you want to push as hard as possible to get your money as fast as possible, but purposely always pay out money as slow as possible. This guarantees that you will always have a larger padding of business money available to do as you please. Consider this general business tactic when you are waiting on your own money. Someone may be doing it to you. As they say, business is business.

Many of us schedule our bill payments for the final due date. If you miss the deadline, you will be charged a fee. With our business, it's a little harder to enforce overdue fees, but you can certainly try. It may anger the client and your next payment may show up even later. It's not just us little guys being stretched out, though. I've sat in meetings with the big corporations and have heard them complain about the same problem. Everyone will wait until the last minute, or forget as long as you don't notice.

Consider rewarding those clients who pay you the fastest. Clients who pay fast show that they respect me and the work I do for them. If they pay me fast, I may certainly try my best to complete their project sooner. We all need some form of motivation, and money can be one of the best types.

I typically work on a 30-day invoice cycle for many of my established clients. All of my invoices state that any past due balances beyond 30 days will result in all current development being stopped until the payments are caught up. This prevents things from getting out of hand. The idiom, "Give an inch and he'll take a mile" should be considered here. Unless you set boundaries, your clients will wait as long as they think they can get away with it. It's just human nature.

Setting a due date is just a way to throttle slow payers. If I were to forget to pay my phone bill or rent what do you think would happen? All of these services would be stopped, I would be thrown out on the streets, and be forced to talk through a soup can tied to a string.

So much of our daily lives consists of passing money from one person to another. As independents, we must become masters at making sure our money ends up in our pockets in a proper time frame. Not getting our money on time could be the difference between our business failing and being able to grow to the next level. If we are always just barely getting our money in time before the bills hit, we will never be able to advance ourselves. It's a vicious cycle that you must break if your clients are always late with their payments.

CHAPTER 21

Startups: Las Vegas for the Hacker

One thing that has always remained the same throughout my experiences: startups will be one big wild ride across the unknown. You can not possibly know what direction they will take on a monthly basis.

Startups take a massive risk while trying to push the world forward. They are the ultimate version of a high stakes casino. I wonder if a study has been done to see the percentage of startup founders and investors that are fond of gambling. How many of them head to Las Vegas, Atlantic City, or Macao on a regular basis? Maybe they find startups less risky than the poker table? I'm no expert on either.

From my own experiences, these are the things that I do know. There will be the good times like when the founders are jetting off to parties at the Playboy mansion, and there will be the bad ones like when you are told to immediately stop all active development because an investor has backed out. There is no more money to continue on, and now they can't even pay anyone for work already completed.

Something you should plainly be aware of with a startup: you are an expendable resource. Startups expect you to devote 100% of yourself to their cause and be a team player. They expect that everyone should work day and night until their product is launched. Once it's launched, they then expect you to continue maintaining it no matter the time or day.

I understand the drive and motivation many people have to want to help change the world. The problem I have with many startups is that you never can truly get comfortable. Unless they have fully convinced you that their company will succeed, you simply can't feel safe about your job. This is probably why startups mostly hire younger candidates. Most of them do not have families or responsibilities to take care of if they lose their job so quickly. Business is business, and a startup's goal may change on a daily basis, so you can never be quite sure what tomorrow will bring for you. You may be needed today, but when their business pivots in a week, what side of the fence will you be on? Will you still be needed?

Honestly, though, I really commend startup founders for the craziness that they go through. Some of them will get the winning lottery ticket, but most of them will crash and burn. Consumers take for granted that amount of innovation we see on a daily basis that was accomplished due to startups. Their founders often risk financial ruin to accomplish their idea, yet stand to profit heavily from a successful startup. Many of these companies are bought out before they ever even take off very far, so you may never actually know who truly came up with that life changing idea.

The best startups understand that the employees are the ones who make their vision happen and will give a much larger reward to the employees because of this. If the founders create a high level of morale with the employees, their company may well be rewarded with an even better version of their vision. Having happier employees could make the difference between a lackluster product versus something jaw-dropping.

Based on my own personal and friend-discussed experiences, I tend to request a majority of my pay from startups be in cash. Only in the smallest number of exceptions will I be willing to work on a tiny percent of equity with the rest being paid in cash. That's how little faith I have in the odds of a startup working out and rewarding their employees properly. No matter how nice and cool the founders may be, the chances that their company will fail is very high. There are a few industries and topics that catch more of my interest, though. If a startup's idea falls into those categories I may take a slight equity. It just has to hit into industries that connect to me somehow.

In no circumstances will I work entirely on equity. I have to eat and pay my bills. I've always heard that going into business with family is one of the worst things you can do. Family related situations can be the hardest ones to say no to for most people when it comes to taking on a "free" project. Thankfully, I've never run into any of those situations myself. Here is an easy explanation to give a family member if they are wanting you to go into business together and you've told them you aren't interested. First and foremost, make them understand that ideas are a dime a dozen. That it's all about execution and the hard work (and likely months) that go into crafting that idea into something usable. They need to understand that if you were to spend months working on their idea, you would have no extra income coming in.

If they still don't understand and seriously want you to work on their idea, tell them that you as the developer deserve 95% of the profits from the idea. That you two should work up a contract for their 5%, and you'd be happy to start the project if they want to front you your portion of the expected profits for the first year. You would gladly then pay them their money back and their 5% cut only if the idea is successful. Or you could go for the most obvious explanation—that if they truly cared for you as a family member or friend, they wouldn't expect you to work for free.

I can only speak from my own experiences and from stories I have been told. It's very possible that there are plenty of people who have worked for the right startups and struck it rich. Think of working with a startup as a high-risk loan you've given out—you may never see your money. My advice is to ask for a guaranteed portion of pay up front and raise your rates higher than you normally charge. There is a chance a startup will fold without notice and you may never see your money.

CHAPTER 22

For-Loop Your Life

Whenever I tell someone that I work from home, the top question I get asked is how do I ever get any work done? They usually say that they *would just sit on their couch and watch TV all day*. With the popularity of social media, others would just sit online all day wasting time. The underwear question is somewhere in the top 10, I swear.

It certainly makes it easier to spend a late night out with the friends knowing that I can just sleep in an extra hour if I need to, but I have rarely ever taken advantage of that. Many of my clients are in an earlier time zone than myself, so I need to be up and ready promptly in the morning. I've also always been a bit more of a morning person and I have a hungry cat, so regardless of what time I go to bed, I am usually up early anyway.

I like to jokingly call myself just a "big walking talking supercomputer" full of software programs. So just like I would try to solve my software projects, I think of myself in the same way. Everything I do is built on how my brain perceives and what commands are given to it. I feel it's important to have a routine that acts as a mental switch. Something that can tell your brain that it is time to work, and then something that tells your brain it is time to stop.

By doing this to myself, I am able to partition off exactly the right amount of time for a work day and then easily shut off my mind when it's necessary. This is obviously not always the case when larger projects arise. Sometimes you will need to give extra hours and additional effort to meet a client's needs, and I will usually try to adjust my routines to match the scheduling. So whenever a scheduling change is necessary, I try to also adjust my mental switches accordingly.

This is why I rely on physical actions rather than set times. My morning mental switch is a nice fast-paced jog or walk through my neighborhood. It helps me wake up, clear my mind, and start setting up my goals for the day.

Quite often the goals I set do not end up all getting accomplished because at least one client usually comes up with an urgent request that must get done as soon as possible. I often try to consider the possibility of these when I am setting my daily goals. Like I've mentioned before, I always try to leave a little room in my day for something unexpected. If nothing ends up happening, I can either call it a day early or I work on something extra like this book.

When my work day is over, I usually go for another jog or walk. This helps me clear my mind from the day's work. The after-work shutdown also sometimes includes a nice hot shower. I personally find showers to be very relaxing as it is a time to quiet your mind and cleanse myself physically and mentally.

I've had some version of a paying job since I was 16, and I did have the benefit of working real office jobs before I went off on my own. All of these experiences allowed me to grow accustomed to the daily 9am-5pm style work schedule. Now, instead of driving to work, I walk or jog my neighborhood. Instead of driving home, I walk or jog my neighborhood as well. This simulates the act of coming to and going from work that an office job would require. Working an office job also gave me experience with the general guidelines I should follow as for my own work hours.

My father was a long-distance runner who broke a few local records in high school. By the time I was born, he was still running in regional road races just for fun, and my family would often travel with him to all of these events. I started entering into races of my own once I became old enough, and ran my first six-mile race when I was eight years old.

Learning how to control my own mind and prevent myself from hitting the "runner's wall" is something I am very thankful for today. It has helped me to understand the nature of how mind over matter works, and understand how to push myself beyond what I believe my body thinks it can handle.

I enjoy trying to hack myself. There, I said it. Some mornings I don't want to get out of bed. Yet, I push myself out regardless. My mind is then really trying to tell me that I do not want to go for a jog or walk, so I begin to bargain with myself in some way to make it happen. As a programmer, we are used to breaking down large tasks into much smaller pieces. Then we figure out a way to make each of those pieces do what they are supposed to do. One by one, they work in unison to complete a task. Breaking down our own psyches to do the same is what must happen. This is something you must master in order to stop yourself from limiting your own success. You must learn to master your mind.

As humans, we tend to feel more comfortable with set routines, and getting us outside of our normal daily plan can cause confusion. By setting my morning and evening routines, I feel that anything that needs to happen in between becomes simpler. Now I have an established block of space that I can use every day with different tasks if necessary.

Lunch in itself is a routine most of us have every day. Our bodies are accustomed to us providing food for energy every day at near the same time. Try to wait an hour longer and notice how your body reacts. Television shows have allowed people to create weekly routines around their schedules. I think we've all either done this ourselves or known someone who wouldn't attend an event because we didn't want to miss our favorite TV show. The DVR has thankfully saved millions of people from being stuck at their home every night.

We as humans are obviously easily programmed into routines. In some ways, this can be bad, like with brain-washing. The important thing is that you create beneficial routines for yourself, and not ones that hold you back. Whatever your goal is, create a daily routine to make it happen. If you must, create a checklist, one that you can re-use every day.

CHAPTER 23

Hours of Operation

I think this is an extremely important lesson that all of us independents need to learn. Working from home makes it extremely easy to keep on working the night away, and sometimes it's difficult to even stop long enough to eat a meal. We get too deep into our current project and clients usually know we are at home.

It's also very easy to return back to work late at night after dinner if an important e-mail or message comes in from a client. There are no physical barriers between your home and your office. Not like most office jobs, where you can leave and be left mostly alone until the next morning.

The truth is that you need to set boundaries. Whether subconsciously or not, some clients will slowly chip away at your business-hour boundaries. They will start to feel it's okay to contact you after business hours and expect you to respond within a short period of time. The occasional urgent request should be expected and sometimes even hoped for. I have previously mentioned before that if you have clearly stated to all of your clients that all urgent requests will cost additional money, then you should be happy to occasionally hear from them after hours. The sad reality, though, is that you are never truly off the clock.

I hear more and more from my friends with office jobs that the above behavior is almost expected now from many corporate salary jobs too. These people work in an office and then are also expected to go home and be available to handle any additional items all through the night. Then, they must go to bed and return back to the office the following day.

At least for me I never have to leave my house. If clients want to bother me day and night, at least I am not additionally tired from travel to and from my office. Plus, I can ask for extra money. Office jobs do not typically offer that option if you are on a salary.

Depending on the company, salary jobs do offer more financial security than someone who works independently. We, as independents, often have to be concerned about our next work feast or famine. Both situations obviously have their own distinct advantages.

The funniest myth I hear people say about working for yourself is that it makes you your own boss and that you do not have to answer to anyone else. This could not be more wrong. In reality, every single client is now your boss. So instead of having one boss like people commonly have at a day job, you now have multiple bosses located in different corners of the world; each with their own requests, desires, and attitudes. With many of them, their business hours may not even match up with your own. You can not possibly set up your own hours to make every client happy if you have ones in various time zones.

My advice is to match your hours closest with the time zone you have the most clients or expect to have the most clients in. Ten years ago, a majority of my clients came from the Eastern Standard Time Zone, but I was in the Pacific Standard Time Zone. That's a three-hour difference in time, so I tried my best to shift my daily schedule earlier so I could better match up their hours.

What I found was that over time, they actually liked the fact that I was a few hours behind them. If something came up at the last minute just before their work day ended, they could still send a request over to me. My day was not quite done yet, so I could make things happen. Eventually, as work dried up from afar, I relaxed my hours to meet what was better for me locally. This meant changing from waking at 4am to being able to sleep in until 6am.

Some clients have a problem meeting their own daily deadlines. Maybe it's from overloading their day with meetings, too much procrastinating, poor management, or something else entirely random. Here's an example of a situation that I see way too often. After a long delay, a client finally gets back to me on something that they need completed by the next morning. It's late afternoon, and now highly likely that I will have to work past my normal hours to get this done. Even if I stopped all other work right now, this deadline will probably not be met. What would you do in this situation?

Here's how I handle it. If it's a client I've had for a while and this behavior isn't typical, then I will try to do my best to complete what they ask. I'd advise requesting a higher billable rate of nearly twice what you normally charge for rush requests like this. This achieves two things: 1) It shows them that your personal time is valuable. 2) It will make some clients think twice about their priorities and make sure they get things to you when they should. In my opinion, they will respect you more in all matters. If it angers a client and they walk away not long after this, then it's probably better for you anyway.

You need to set the tone that they can not expect you to be on call every day to complete their tasks. If they truly wanted you to be available all day every day, then they would be paying you a daily or weekly rate. You may be working on something for somebody else, and it would reflect badly on you if you were to always be dropping everyone else for a client who clearly has no respect for you.

If a new potential client's project is needed so urgently that they want to make me drop everything else and rush to complete it, they are not a good candidate for someone I want to work with long-term. Especially if it's something large enough that I may possibly need to even work on over the weekend. That's a big red flag to me. Obviously, trust your own gut instinct in situations like this. If there is a potential for long-term work with someone, and this seems like an exception, then you should consider giving them a pass. Just this one time, though.

I used to take projects like this on fairly often in my earlier days because I believed that these companies had the potential to give me additional projects in the future. I regarded their rush projects as a chance to "prove myself" to them, and I threw away my normal business hours to make sure their projects were completed. Only a tiny percentage of them ever turned into anything else. Maybe these people had been holding out for other developers that never panned out or became available. Now, they only had a few short days before they told their own boss the project would be done. So they find me, I complete what they needed, and that was that. I rarely heard from most of these types ever again.

The few that I did were for almost the exact same scenarios. It's as if I was their fireman; they only ever came to me when it was urgent. I could usually tell that other work had been done since my last project was completed for them. So who had been working on those other tasks? Where did they go?

Situations like these are why I tend to turn down rush projects from clients I barely know. You don't know the history of the situation and how it came to be so terribly managed. Would your local supermarket stay open an extra hour later if you show up late because you forgot to put gas in your car? Will the movie theater delay the start of a movie because you forgot what time it started? That's not the theater's problem. Neither should it be mine to help someone who has poor project management skills.

As always, if you decide to continue to be someone's emergency service, charge a much higher price than you normally would. Just like how emergency rooms charge a much higher price than your regular medical doctors. Your time should be valuable. Make these people understand that if they are coming to you in a pinch, you have to be rewarded for saving their asses.

Set your hours and stick to them. If anyone wants you to work on something, you'll be available only during that time frame every day. If they want something extra, then so do you. Have respect for yourself.

CHAPTER 24

Easier Said Than Done

Whether it's subconscious or deliberate, anyone who says their project is easy is probably after lowball prices. What they really mean is, "While we can't personally do this particular piece of code ourselves, it seems extremely easy to explain so it must be simple. Anyone with even the most basic level of programming should be able to knock this one out in their sleep. It's easy money. Breeze through it in a few minutes, and we'll pay you less than the price of a latte."

No project is ever really as easy as someone can explain it. Otherwise, people wouldn't need to hire a software expert. Certainly someone's level of experience may make a project take a shorter length of time than someone who is brand new to a situation.

For me, this translates into per hour billable rates. If someone is entry level or new to a programming language or situation, it may take them more time to learn how to do a particular task. These individuals may charge a smaller per hour rate to compensate for the fact that they are less experienced at this situation or language. A more experienced programmer who has mastered a situation or language will typically take much less time to create the needed code. This experienced programmer can charge a higher rate for a shorter period of time.

Ultimately, both types of programmers may be able to complete the same project, and it's a possibility that both received about the same amount of money for finishing the task. One just took longer than the other to do the job. Eventually, the entry level programmer will become experienced, and can then charge the higher rate for future projects relating to the same language or situation.

Many clients, especially people who are new to needing programmers, will seek out the less experienced programmers because they know they are cheaper. They will generally say, "Why would I pay two to three times the price that I would for someone else?" This can be understandable if the supposed experienced programmer does not live up to the example I mentioned above and actually takes longer than the less experienced and cheaper programmer.

The problem with clients labeling their project as simple or easy is that they gauge their task from how long they think it would take an expert to complete their project, yet want to pay the entry level price. Usually, this time measurement is even shorter than the true time even an expert could complete it in.

Either the person's ego has gotten in the way or they are truly that blind to reality.

My advice would be to not short-change yourself. Stick to what price you feel is correct for yourself. If a client will not agree to that price, then consider walking away. Tell them that if they change your mind within the next 30 days (or something similar), your are still willing to work for the estimated price you gave.

What about past clients who have a solid record for being honest, but now claim to have a really easy project they need your help with? Situations like these can be hard. While you have a past relationship with this client, that by no means forces you to continue working with them in the future. Unless a contract is in place, either one of you can walk away at any time.

If a past client said this to me, I would not believe them. We are all business people; I get that. We all want to push and pull enough to possibly squeak out a little more money for ourselves. Maybe this is their way of trying to squeeze a few more dollars out of your pocket by keeping it in their own a little longer?

First off, ask for as much clarification as you can. Do not leave the details of the project open or vague. If it's something they need with a quick turnaround, make sure your contract states that a more exact estimate figure will be given as more details of the project are in your hands. When you respond back with your estimate, you could also include an extra amount of dollars to compensate for the unknowns.

If it's a corporate client who tends to have lots of employees, always consider that there will be multiple people with differing opinions on the project. This factor may greatly affect the outcome of the project. With too many people all trying to have their say, it could cause things to spin out of control. So while a simple project might be the beginning description, there is a large chance that the end result will be nothing similar to the original description. So many people have offered suggestions that the project has gone off scope, and it's become something else entirely.

Thankfully, smaller clients usually only have a few people offering their opinions. But always remember that no matter how small the company is, the average project manager or business owner does not understand what truly goes on behind the scenes in code. From the visual side, a site may look like another, but that's where it ends. Each site may use completely different languages and frameworks, animations, layout actions, and more.

Clients sometimes will ask that you simply copy the look of another site. To them, it sounds easy enough. That it's probably not too much different than just hitting the copy and paste keys. So they contact you about this project, label it as easy, and then want an estimate for you to get it done.

Often, their initial details do sound simple enough. You have a sample site to use as a visual example (the site they want you to copy), so you give a fairly straightforward estimate. Then the full details start to trickle in. They want to change multiple parts of this copied site, many of which need entirely new sets of design and code.

Further requests are then asked that require massive chunks to be removed from the old site. By the time you are done, this copied site looks nothing like the original one. You have just been bamboozled. They got the "copy a website" cheap price out of you, but ultimately wanted something entirely new and original. Instead of telling you this from the beginning and receiving a proper estimate for the right price, they got it for a lot cheaper than it should have been.

So what's the bottom line here? Simple and easy projects are usually anything but that, and as usual always have a contract in place. If your contract is more of an open-ended hourly rate with estimate situations, be very straightforward. After every new request out of scope, respond back that these changes are beyond your estimate.

Take notes and be very descriptive. If their original details outlined that they only wanted you to copy a site, but they are now adding in new sections, state this. List out all of the areas that they have requested to be different to the original, and become the thorn in their side after every request. You are only protecting yourself. Simple project or not, you just want to squeeze out the few more dollars for yourself that you deserve.

CHAPTER 25

Surviving the Blame Game

It became apparent to me that some clients may possibly enjoy causing conflict. Maybe they are overworked, over stressed, or scared of business failure. It's also possible that some personalities do not work well together. Maybe something about me irritates them and we spiral into terrible situations because of this. The hardest type of clients to work for will applaud you on the amazing things you do for them one minute, and then degrade you in an e-mail the next minute. These e-mails will be full of comments like, "What did you do to the site? You must have broke it!". It gets very confusing.

This is a hard situation to solve. It's even more difficult when you are working with someone else's legacy code. Maybe the client really loved working with their previous consultant, but for whatever reason, that consultant is now gone.

Sometimes you inherit a website with a previous

programmer's outdated code and must make sense of what they left behind. This can make me feel like an archaeologist when I am trying to look through this old code. The same goes for even my own old code. You can often see how the trends were at the time, like what plugins were available back then and which ones didn't exist yet. You can also possibly determine how advanced the programmer was when they wrote it.

I have one very old client who still calls me about once a year for very minor changes to code I wrote for them over ten years ago. They have no interest in redoing any of this code base. It's all internal applications that helps them parse very old data file types from another piece of software. Every year or so, these report files change a tiny amount, so they need me to make slight adjustments to my code to compensate.

It's "easy" for me to make these changes, but it's also a little embarrassing when I open up the code and look at my own work from over 10 years ago. It may have very well been good code for that period of time, but wow, how have times changed. Not only has my skills improved, but coding standards have also shifted. Quicker solutions are certainly available now, but sadly this client is very adamant about their needs. Their message to me is always the same, "Just make the new change, and invoice us. See you next year!". So I bite my tongue a little and then just make the change. I leave the cobwebs the way they were and go about my business elsewhere.

I have often heard from other programmers that if you look at your old code and do not cringe a little, you are not improving yourself enough.

Back to the lesson at hand. Let's be honest—some people live their lives as the constant victim. These types of people generally believe that a problem is always someone else's fault. If you have a client that blames their previous consultant for most of their problems, it should be a huge red flag to you. Because, guess what? You will probably be the next person blamed for everything going wrong. It probably won't be to your face, but once you are also gone, you can bet your favorite hooded sweatshirt that you will be blamed for anything wrong with the code.

Once you begin handling new tasks for this client, everything will now be your fault. An item you fixed may not even be on the same website as something that breaks, but somehow, what you did is the cause of the issue. My favorite is when items that were already broken long before you came around are only noticed after you make an unrelated change.

So was this client paying so little attention to their site before that they weren't even noticing these old issues? Now that you are actively working on new things for them, they are now paying more attention to the site. So it's only now that they see the problems, and it must all be your fault since they had never seen anything wrong before.

So how do you handle these situations? It's usually difficult enough to explain to a client how code actually works. It's even harder when they have convinced themselves it is your fault and are blaming you for everything wrong. I've tried backing up my explanations with facts, code samples, and anything else to prove it. My results have varied.

Even after making a change, and they notice the problem has gone away, they will still blame you. You simply fixed something that you previously broke. Many of these clients will even expect that these fixed items are not billable. It's like buying something from a department store when it was already broken. You should be able to get your money back or the store will replace it with something else. You, as the customer, aren't charged anything additional. In the client's mind, you as the provider should merely make your customers happy by fixing something you previously broke.

Maybe I am a little jaded from clients like these, and I have had to walk away from a few of them after my project ended. It was simply obvious that we were not going to work well together. From my own experiences, you just can not change this type of behavior. I certainly hope you have better luck dealing with these types than I did. Maybe this is why some other programmers I know refuse to work on legacy code projects? They will only work on brand new sites from scratch.

So I have two options that I would consider. Option 1: The easy way out. Complete anything you are currently under contract to do. Hold back your tongue, meditate, and do whatever it takes to survive this situation. Then simply become too busy to work on their projects anymore. Kindly tell them that they need to find someone else to handle any further requests. Or Option 2: When your fiscal year hits, announce that you are raising your rates for all clients. It will either make their pain easier to bear or make them move on to the next person to blame.

I highly recommend that you document everything you do for them. You want to make sure that they do not attempt to come back at you later with a lawsuit that is trying to blame you for something you clearly did not do. You just never know how far these types of personalities will go to try and blame you for their own woes.

CHAPTER 26

Reading Their Minds

I will have to admit that the following situations probably irritate me much easier than they should. Sometimes clients just seem to lack an acceptable level of business etiquette. Certainly, clients who blame you for everything do usually lack this trait. Some people just lack the common sense required to handle situations properly. It's the little condescending comments and the attitude they show during your conversations.

For example, say a client gives you a mock-up or prototype design for a new website that they wish for you convert into workable code. There's typically a conference call or an in-office meeting to go over the details and answer any questions you might have. Once that is complete, you then create a version as close as code can possibly come to a design file. You seem fairly confident that this is what they desire, and then send it to the client.

Their response is loaded with insulting phrases about how you got it entirely wrong, they were expecting something better, and completely different. Their words sound as if you managed to create something so terribly off from what they wanted, and it is entirely your fault for not understanding their needs. Sometimes clients will send you a mock-up that is just supposed to be a starting point and expect you to read their mind. They use cryptic comments like *"you need to fix this"* instead of *"you need to change this"*. To me, *"fix"* implies that I did something wrong. *"Change"* implies that it is an adjustment to something they requested.

When a request is different than the example that was originally sent to me, it is a change not an error. The important point here is that the client may be trying to get around paying you extra money. A fix is just something you did wrong, while a change could be outside of the contract scope and would be a new billable item. If it's something I clearly made a mistake on, then yes, it is a fix.

I know I am splitting hairs on this one, but these types of people make my work less enjoyable. I do my best to try and confirm every single little item before I begin. Sometimes, I may even ask so many questions that it annoys the client. I just want things to go as smoothly as possible.

Sometimes, they never bother to tell you that the plans have changed. Suddenly, the design I used as my basis was not entirely what they were planning to use. They wanted to alter it afterward but never bothered to tell me. Whether they knew before I started or after, it's still a change to them. What I did was not right and somehow I should have known.

Indecisive clients can eat your time up very quickly. Doing this type of thing to me is not a full show-stopper, but it's something to look out for. Especially if it keeps happening.

Another item that shows inexperience and makes it rough to deal with is when clients like to use wrong or vague terminology when they are explaining things to you. Anyone that has ever worked in customer support knows how hard it is to deduce exactly what someone means.

Some clients will use outdated phrases or even create new terminology with their own meaning. These can all make it difficult to understand exactly what someone wants. Sometimes you can even deal with very vague error descriptions from clients that weren't actually errors at all; they were just having difficulties using their own products.

The final item here is the ever constant *"moving target"*. These are clients that start out with a very vague idea for a project. You attempt to clarify what it is they want you to do, then describe it back to them, and come to a mutual understanding of what they need. Everything gets confirmed and a contract is signed. You enter into development and then finally *complete* the project. This is only when the fun begins.

Request after request starts to fill your inbox. "This didn't turn out how I thought it would. I actually meant for you to do it this other way. This is just Phase 1, there are 2 more phases." All of these are signs that the client really has no idea what they wanted. It becomes apparent that no clear plan was ever set up before development started or you were only told part of the plan. They had decided to withhold additional details from you.

Sometimes clients just really don't know what they want. Maybe they had an idea, but didn't know how to properly execute it. Their idea just continues to evolve as they get a better understanding of what it is they believe they want to achieve.

Sadly, some clients also don't even understand their own business well enough to give you clear directions. Some never even use their own websites. You may end up spending more time trying to explain to them how to use their own website than you spend on actual work. You end up going in circles on items that you have already discussed, having to explain it all to them again in the future. They may not even even remember discussing it with you before.

I like to keep notes from conference calls and then send my "to do" list to my clients afterward in an e-mail. This way they can confirm what we discussed on the phone. Every now and then, I will get some clients who will ask questions about the items on my list. They themselves don't remember what it is they wished for me to do.

I know this chapter sounds a little nitpicky, but being proactive in one's own business tends to be a clear sign of whether that business will succeed or not. If I'm too busy trying to educate clients on their own websites, businesses, or on simple procedures that most popular websites use then I will never be able to get anything done for them. Then they will get angry because I am behind on development.

I will give my usual advice: always have contracts and only work on hourly rates. If you must do fixed amounts, outline exactly what is included in that price. Anything additional means more negotiated money. It's not your fault they didn't think this through. My power to read minds was misplaced.

CHAPTER 27

Pacing Your Clients

Sometimes clients come to you with urgent projects that need to be done in a very short period of time. Maybe a new product has launched or they completely forgot to tell you about it, and now their boss is yelling at them. These are never ideal situations, but maybe this particular client has usually been good about paying you on time and urgent requests aren't a normal occurrence for them.

There are a few things you can do to make sure that this task goes as best as it possibly can. First off, raise your price to your urgent request rate. Make sure the client realizes that this project will be at a higher rate. You do not want them to come back to you later on with questions as to why your bill is much higher than they expected it to be. You can also attempt to request a deposit up front, but it is unlikely that a money transfer will happen that fast. They desperately need the project to be done right now. You could accept a quick payment through services like Square, Paypal, or even Bitcoin. These are all fast payment methods, but there may be a hefty fee involved.

The second thing you should do is spend an hour understanding exactly what it is they need you to do and when is their deadline. Make sure to get at least an e-mail confirmation for what exactly they need you to do. I like using e-mails as a form of record keeping. Verbals over the phone can be forgotten, misinterpreted, or downright lied about. I also use Slack, Wunderlist, and Jira for various requests.

The third thing I recommend is that you plan out your work schedule and hold yourself to it. Do not overwork yourself. It's not your fault that their project is in urgent mode. Yes, they can hire someone else in the future if you don't work fast enough for them, but do you really want to continue working with someone who holds you responsible for their own actions?

The fourth and final recommendation is to make sure that you have all of your other tasks under control. This may seem a little obvious, but going so deep into this project may cause you to forget about your own needs. I once didn't leave the inside of my apartment for 7 straight days while trying to get a project done. Make sure your refrigerator is full and try to limit the amount of food you have delivered. It can get pricey.

Now that you are ready to begin, chain yourself to your desk for the next several days, and get things done. If a question comes up, never ever assume you know the answer. Double-check with the client about questionable items, even if it slows you down a little. This downtime could be used for a nap, meal, your first shower, or something else.

So, now you've completed the project. Happy that you were able to meet the deadline, you contact the client with a large grin on your face. Hours go by and no one responds. Days go by and you still haven't heard anything. Finally, they get back to you with a vague excuse, nothing has still been launched, and they've barely even commented on your work. Days turn into weeks and finally a month later they announce that they plan to launch it. You have just busted your ass for nothing.

Don't be too hard on yourself. You did set your inflated payment rate correctly, right? A cautious warning, though, the client may try to say that the project should no longer be considered urgent since it wasn't launched for a month. Make sure to state clearly in your current contract that urgent requests are charged based upon the day they were developed, not on the project end date. If the client complains any further, it may be reason enough to walk away. Let's make it clear. When I say walk away, I of course mean after you have been paid.

What can you do about situations like this? Not much. You can attempt to confirm over and over with a client that this due date is for real and not just a hopeful completion date. It probably won't really mean too much, though, and they may always try to change their words. This is why I recommend getting it in a contract or at least in some form of record that you can bring back up later on.

Ultimately, the only thing you can do is make sure to boost your pay to equal the stress you put yourself under. If the client questions this, it's probably a sign that you should say no to the project anyway. If they can't understand their own ridiculousness, then move along.

CHAPTER 28

Following the Trends

Many of us would like to believe we are true independent thinkers—we like to see ourselves as someone who goes against the expected path. We choose to follow our own instincts and do things how we want to do them, regardless of whether it is truly beneficial to us or not. We want to believe that our principles and integrity outweigh any actual benefit we can gain from "going with the flow".

This may make you feel exceptional in your own head, but the reality is that none of us are special snowflakes. We are all on this same planet together. Why is it that during a particular year, every major pop music song sounds similar? This same basic idea holds true in most parts of the world. Ever listened to K-Pop? Many of their songs all sound the same.

The general public as a collective does not want to think too hard about something. Collectively, things should just fall in line.

But that's not you! You consider yourself unique and a free-thinker. You read obscure books (like this one), and watch only films from the deepest of underground independent filmmakers. You would not be spotted in public wearing the same fashion as everyone else, and you certainly would not be caught dead listening to that generic bubblegum pop music found on your Top 40 radio station.

This may be an okay way to live your personal life. By all means, try to be unique. The problem lies with acting this way in your business. A good business strives off what is currently popular as well as what will be popular. So good independent software developer can also benefit from being experienced in the latest trending languages and templates.

Just a few years ago, changing from marketing myself as primarily a PHP engineer to a Django engineer increased my level of new client interest dramatically. I usually re-analyze my marketing tactics every 6-8 months.

I know I've previously said that it isn't necessarily good to just hop onto whatever programming language is popular at the moment. That isn't what I am saying to do here. I prefer to let things settle for a while before I jump on board with it. I don't catch it during the first wave, but I still manage to catch it on its way up the popularity ladder. It's best to catch something once it has gained enough popularity and ride it higher, than to jump on too soon and waste your time when it never takes off.

But what about actual business trends? Many businesses

target specific groups of people. Some businesses and individuals are really good at telling individual groups exactly what they want to hear, accumulating all of these groups individually, and then bringing them all together.

It's like catering to each group of people separately in order to gain them as new customers, but making sure you are not angering any of your other groups in the process. The general public, when all lumped together, can follow a pretty bland trend line. Formulaic pop music that all sounds the same, chain restaurants that try to make their food generic enough that it caters to everyone, and clothing trends that when looked at objectively are downright hilarious.

The iPhone came out and then suddenly kiosk after kiosk popped up selling phone cases. There may be 3-4 kiosks in a shopping mall selling the same cases. These are all examples of ways companies just follow what are believed to be trends.

If a new sound becomes hot on the music scene, within a few months, several other songs will come out that sound the same. Now that artisan style hamburgers are popular in the US, every chain restaurant is trying to copy their buzz and serve them too. Most of the chain restaurants miss entirely what it is that makes them so popular though. A celebrity gets photographed wearing a certain style of jeans, and shortly afterward, every jeans company has copied that look.

So how do these companies know exactly what it takes to reel in new customers? This all comes from substantial amounts of market research. Some companies use fear to draw in customers, knowing that if they spin their story perfectly enough the right demographic will latch onto them. Often, people will believe these stories without even questioning the validity of what the business is saying. Common industries that use this tactic include dietary supplement and alternative medicine companies. It's believed that many of them prey on people desperate for a cure.

Even I, during my own health scares, found that I was willing to give everything a shot. When none of the common methods are working, people are willing try anything. Many of the claims on the bottles from these companies have no scientific basis. It's truly just business to them. It's possible some of these products do actually work, but it's a good bet that many of them don't even contain the ingredients listed.

Tricking your customers can eventually catch up with you, and I personally wouldn't recommend it. Other businesses just do exactly what the market research says the general public wants. For them, it just becomes a numbers game. If something is extremely popular, the company that follows an exact trend will have plenty of opportunities to succeed if they execute their plans properly.

My example of iPhone case kiosks is a prime example of this. I don't see how running a kiosk full of phone cases could be exciting, but it may very well be profitable if you have the right products.

Following the Trends

On the surface, the larger trends all seem boring to me. My inner personality that wants to be unique and different is screaming to run far away from such things. But I am also a business person, so deep down, I know the game. Going with the flow allows you the opportunity to make money, and it allows you to set your sights on where you see the wave heading.

I've known many business people that do not even really believe in what they are selling. Sometimes they even know that the product doesn't do what it says it will. Or it could simply be in an industry or genre that they really couldn't care less about. All they care about is that there is a large enough audience for it somewhere out there and they want to grab on to those customers.

The bottom line is that you as a business-minded person should have a full understanding of what the trends are doing in your line of business. Then you should be able to see where you could fit in.

Do you want to provide a niche product that works in conjunction with the trends? Or do you want to follow the exact trends, competing against every other business person in the same line of products? Or finally, do you take door number 3 with the unknown style of products, so unique that only a small group of people may know of their existence? It's your time and your business. Run it the way you feel is best.

CHAPTER 29

Accepting Business Evolution

At the beginning of this book, I mentioned that remote freelancing is an ever-growing area of work for people in various industries. That as the Internet continues to grow in size and availability, the scope of freelancing possibilities will only continue to expand into industries that have yet to allow remote workers. Part of the reason for the constant growth in remote opportunities is that it allows anyone from anywhere to hire another person from somewhere else in the world.

Before the Internet, you were only limited to hiring from the few people in your area who have seen your newspaper classified advertisement or through word of mouth. Now, I can use the Internet to seek out someone who is an expert at a particular task I need completed regardless of their physical location. Or maybe even I can be the professional that someone is seeking out from across a grand distance.

Outsourcing work to another country has been a hotbed topic in the US for many years now. To some, it's a cheaper way of having a task completed. To others, it is hurting our economy. We're sending our money over to people in another country, while workers perfectly capable of doing the work here in the US are left underemployed. My opinion on the topic has changed several times over the years as I've gone from overworked to underemployed myself.

During a number of these underemployed times, I've looked into placing myself on many of the freelancing websites. If you have never used any of them, basically someone needing a task completed will post details about what exactly they need to have done. Freelancers who believe they can complete the task will all bid on this project. Some of the bids will be very well-documented while others will just be a canned response from a team in a developing country. Examples of these types of sites include: Freelancer.com, PeoplePerHour.com, 99designs.com, and UpWork.com.

Some of these sites limit the number of projects freelancers can bid on during a specific period of time. This helps to block developer teams from bidding low on every single project listed. It's a somewhat effective method of watching out for quality control, and people who purchase memberships have the ability to bid on a much larger number of projects every month.

As an engineer in the US who was once desperate for work, I could have easily become disheartened from what people were bidding on these sites. The cost of living here in the US is much higher than in a number of the developing countries I would see bids coming from. There is absolutely no way I could have ever competed with the bids that most of these people were offering. Many of the people posting projects were just choosing the lowest bidders.

We can all come up with opinions on why they would choose the lowest bidders. The obvious answer is simply that the bidder was the cheapest and the client wanted to save money. The client could also be very inexperienced and have no idea why one person would want to charge more than another.

Like I mentioned before, many of these low bidders wouldn't even bother to mention anything directly related to the project itself. They would just list out details of past projects they have worked on. It was obvious that they were playing the numbers game. They know they can get away with paying no real attention to what the project is about, and someone will still choose them because they bid so little money.

It's possible they are even counting on the people who choose them to be very inexperienced. I have heard stories of these developer teams winning bids only to under-deliver and then try to up-sell better services to complete the task properly.

I myself wanted to initially hate these developer teams. I despised that they could offer to complete a project for 1/10th of the price I would bid. But then I started thinking of situations like this differently. I was probably better off that these people did not choose me since they decided on such a lower bid. Or maybe they held chat sessions with these people and found that they were as legit as anyone could be.

What I started realizing was that there will always be people who want the cheapest rate regardless of quality, but there will be other people who look beyond prices and solely for the right person(s) for the job. I have actually communicated with other engineers who have solid incomes coming from these websites. These engineers are charging prices more in line with my own US rates. Many of them use their specialties to assist in their bidding and focusing on technologies not as often found in the developing countries. In general, you have to keep pushing until you eventually meet people more tuned in to your abilities.

I do still bid on projects from time to time, and have noticed that these websites run heavily on past ratings. If you have never completed a project on a particular website before, you may find it more difficult to land your first project. You will more than likely have to lower your expected pay rates for the first few projects to compete for someone's attention.

Be descriptive in your bid. Mention their project name in a way that signals that you've actually read their description, and you will be a responsive provider. But in no way should you be overly thorough in your bid details. You don't want to waste too much of your time on one bid, but you do want them to know you are paying attention. You need them to feel your experience through your short bid details. If they still decide on someone else, try again on another project. Eventually, you will have enough project experience to earn the rate you feel is right for you.

I have also used these websites from other side—as someone needing to hire people for a wide range of services. These people have come from all over the world. Some have done a better job than others, but I wouldn't say that any one area of the world has been better for me than another. Whether we want to admit it or not, cost is always a factor. This is why I don't fully get angry at other people who always select the lowest bidders. When I select who I will hire, however, I do so based on a few factors.

By being both a provider and seller of freelancing services on these sites, I can get a feel for both sides of the coin. This helps me understand what each side might be thinking. When I am posting a listing, I know to be very thorough in my project details to thin out those who aren't matching my needs. And when I want to find work, I myself have a better understanding as to what looks good so I can submit a better bid. By doing this, I feel it can hopefully help me land a project when I need to do so.

There are other types of websites out there besides those that only offer project bidding. Sites like Fiverr.com allow programmers and other freelancers to list an exact service they will offer and for how much it will cost. If it isn't obvious enough, the name Fiverr.com came from five, as in $5. I believe that originally, every service or task on the site would cost $5, but I think this limitation has been changed now.

Freelancers can also list their services in bulk amounts to increase the prices too. If you needed something done 10 times, you could charge $50 or possibly even a little less since they are buying it in bulk. I, personally, have never offered my services on Fiverr.com. There is really nothing I would want to offer for $5. The tasks can all be fairly simple, while do some seem ridiculously cheap to someone like myself with the cost of living here in the US. I believe overall, this website is targeting workers in developing countries and possibly people (including teenagers) looking for some side work to gain experience.

Similar to this website is Amazon's Mechanical Turk. Like Fiverr, you can list what types of tasks you would offer for a set price. On the flip side, someone needing a task done can list what that task is and what price they are willing to pay someone to do it.

Where the site differs, though, is that these tasks can be as cheap as only a few pennies. Do you need someone to call the doctor's office for you? You can pay someone 5 cents to handle that for you. Say you would like to know the name of a background actor from a particular movie, but don't care to research it on your own. You could post this as a task for a few pennies and someone would likely do it for you. A service provider can also list these types of services on their profile if someone is looking for a specific person to do their tasks for them.

Another website that is a little more open-ended that you can use to connect with people is Reddit. Overall, Reddit is one giant message forum. About any topic you can imagine has its own specific forum on Reddit.

Two forums that can come in handy to find or give work are ForHire and SlaveLabour. ForHire in recent times seems to be more saturated than it was a few years ago, and may be much harder to find work through now. I see so many more programmers using it now to look for work. SlaveLabour is somewhat like Mechanical Turk. You can list a specific task you need done and people will comment about their interest. You can take the conversations private to figure out what they want to charge. Some people on SlaveLabour will list exactly what they will pay for the task.

As someone wanting to give services, you would list exactly what you can do for someone, and what you want to be paid. The name SlaveLabour, does in fact explain itself. I have used Reddit to both find work and other helpers. Overall, I have had a pretty good success with it from both sides.

Another very different type are those that act as your headhunter service. Websites like these act as facilitators to obtain talent from around the world. They often boast that they only have the best of the best software engineers. If a company needed a specific type of programmer, the person that they give you will be one of the best in the world in that specific technology.

These websites put their programmers through a series of tests. I have heard that many of these tests are actually real chunks of code that the company needs someone to do. You as the programmer will usually not be paid for your work, but they may end up billing their clients for that chunk of code when it's connected with other pieces of code. You are basically working for free to see if you are good enough for their website.

I have never worked through any of these types of sites. I have been asked by a couple of them to apply to their sites, and at one point I did start the process. When I got to the part of the process where they wanted me to prove myself by writing real code for free, I declined.

Some of these companies will also require live timed tests. I'm probably just too much of an old timer, but I'm not interested in conducting timed tests to prove myself. They do not prove anything valuable to me. Sure you may be rushed on certain projects, but these types of situations are ridiculous. I do hear that this is becoming quite the standard for bigger companies today, and there are entire websites devoted to helping people practice for these types of tests. This just reiterates what I've been saying all along. The software industry is growing at a very fast rate and becoming extremely competitive.

From the experiences I have heard, most programmers are turned down by these headhunter companies. It's very likely I would have been turned down too. I have also heard that they expect the best in the world but will not pay what the best actually deserves to receive. It's just typical business tactics to me, though, and I am not surprised.

Young and eager people who are brilliant programmers may not yet have the experience to know how good they really are. These engineers may also simply come from developing countries whose cost of living is much lower than the corporations that are hiring them. This makes these types of services very attractive to companies here in the US. Hire the best available engineers in the world, while paying less than you would for your entry level in-office developer. If this bothers you at all, just remember what I've said before, "find the right people who understand your worth".

Globalization will continue to make services easier to reach at cheaper prices. There is simply no way we can compete with these low bid prices. We must learn to work different angles.

CHAPTER 30

Outsourcing the Dilemma

After I finished writing the last lesson, I decided that a more thorough look at my experiences with outsourcing would be good to include. This topic brings up such heated debates among business owners and employees here in the US. Some feel it is the equivalent to stealing jobs from US-based people, while others see it as just part of the ever-growing globalization that is going on in the technology industries.

Eventually, I understood that I needed to accept the direction the trend was heading, and learn how I could harness the situation. I began to grasp the fact that I, too, need not always do all of the work by myself. Throughout all of my years in programming and running my websites, I have hired a number of people to help me. This includes developers, designers (print and web), attorneys, paralegals, publicity, marketing, writers, and various forms of assistants. Most of them I have never met in person.

A number of these people have come from right here in the US, and some of them were even local to me in Los Angeles. The rest have been from all over the world. Most of these people were professionals, while others were newer to their respective industries and just trying to gain some experience. This even includes college students. All of these people have been discovered through a range of methods including Craigslist, Reddit, referrals, word of mouth, and more.

This isn't always the easiest route to find someone though. Sometimes it is quicker to post listings on freelancing websites like I mentioned before. I usually do this when I am extremely busy or having a hard time finding someone who is an expert on a particular topic. Posting on these websites can be faster since it reaches a wider range of people almost instantly. There are a number of drawbacks and headaches you should consider when you use these bidding websites, though.

Many times, I receive such an overwhelming amount of responses from bidders that it becomes a chore just to sift through all of them. I know that sounds like a good problem to have, but sometimes I would almost need to hire someone just to go through all of the bids. Depending on what it is exactly you need help with, there could be hundreds of bidders. After a while, I started getting better at posting projects in a way that would make it easier to find the right person faster.

By being as thorough and exact as possible in my project

details, it causes two things to happen. Many companies will simply search for keywords, and if your project contains that word, they will post a very generic bid. They give just enough information to get you interested in them. These bids typically look so generic that you know quite obviously that these people didn't really bother to read your project. That's an easy indicator for me to just eliminate them now. If they can't pay attention to my details now, they certainly won't do it when we are working on something together.

Secondly, your own thoroughness should inspire people to give their own thorough bid in response. Again, like I mentioned in the last chapter, do not expect them to spell out every single detail about how they plan to solve your problem. Do expect them to give just enough information that you feel that they at least thought about your needs and have given a solid response.

Sometimes in the middle of my details, I will go as far as to tell them to mention a certain exact phrase in their bid response. This may sound like something from a grade school playground where you ask someone for the secret password, but this is a simple a way to know if the bidder truly understands my project. I will then know who fully read my details and who didn't.

Other key questions I like to ask myself while looking through bids: did they explain how they would solve my problem? Did they list examples of how they have accomplished this solution in the past? I also look at their rating to see how other people have rated their service.

Sometimes I consider whether it is a team of people or just one person. Will my project be divided between multiple people who have different coding styles? This can sometimes lead to incoherent code that doesn't always work well together. I've actually had this happen in the past. Thankfully, as a programmer myself, I can go in and fix all of the issues I find after the fact. So it's easier for me gamble and hire a team than someone who has no programming ability themselves.

A bidder's inability to speak perfect English is not something that will stop me from hiring them. If I am able to understand what they are trying to say, and it's clear they understand what my needs are, it won't prevent me from hiring them. I often try to look at it from the other side. The fact that they are able to speak as much of my language as they can is something that I give them credit for doing. It shows motivation and determination; two traits I appreciate. Unless it's some broken Mandarin Chinese or pieces of Spanish, I can't really communicate in any other language. Why should I expect them to be fluent in mine?

Now that you have chosen your team of outsourced help, how do you make sure that things will go as smoothly as possible? It's important to remember the cultural differences between your home country and the people you are hiring. Understand that your country's trends and pop culture will not match up with their's.

Over the years, it has become extremely clear to me that I must make sure I am very meticulous with every detail about my projects. I need to make sure I cover every angle and leave nothing for them to question. Often times, these developers won't want to ask you questions. Sometimes this is down to cultural reasons, in other cases it could be their pride. They don't want to look less talented to you than they originally appeared or they simply want to save face. They may even take it upon themselves to create a solution for something that you did not ask them to do. Once the site is done and you see it for the first time, you may be in for a surprise. How did they possibly come up with what you are seeing from the details you gave?

Their language skills can certainly be part of the flaw as well, as it possible that they may interpret your words entirely different than what you meant. For this reason, I try to keep my details in as basic English as I can. This helps to prevent as many confusions as possible before they ever get the chance to occur.

My documentation to them is always very thorough and as detailed as I can possibly make it. I basically architect the entire project in details and hand-sketched drawings before I send it over to them. They shouldn't have to think too hard about what it is they need to do for me. Even if the people seem to be very smart and quite capable of figuring this all out on their own, my time and money are valuable enough to me to not take any additional chances.

If you are considering using an outsourced designer to create a logo for you, I would advise researching the logos they send in any mock-ups. The sheer level of distance can make it easier for them to rip-off logos far away from you, and you would never know the difference. You may end up paying money for an already created logo that someone else is also using. This may never be a problem for you if none of your customers are international, but once you cross international borders you may be in for embarrassment and possible legal problems.

I often notice that what we in the US consider good web design and user interface designs, doesn't always match up with the trends currently in other countries. This should seem a little obvious, but sometimes you may forget this. Just like what clothes are considered fashionable here, may not be as cool when you go somewhere else. If you aren't careful, your website will look and perform nothing like what you are expecting.

I would advise researching popular websites in your team's country in order to have a better understanding for what they see on a daily basis. You should always include links to sample websites that you want to use as the basis for your own designs. Also, consider sending links for code samples as well to explain how you expect certain features of your website to behave. This way you can have a better chance of receiving something that looks and behaves like what you are envisioning in your mind. You'd be surprised just how much user interface trends differ between countries.

One of the most difficult aspects of outsourcing is how you deal with the difference in time zones. Some international developers will match their work days to yours in order to make it easier for you, but do not expect most of them to do this. Depending on where you are in the world compared to them, you may end up only getting one chance per day to respond to their messages while they are still working. Then they are working on your project while you sleep, and you may wake up the next morning to a wide range of messages and questions. This can be jarring at times and can greatly hinder the speed of your project.

If you are truly dedicated to what it is you are outsourcing, it would ideal for you to always make yourself available as late in your evening as is necessary for them to get their messages to you. Most of the popular messenger programs have mobile applications that can do push notifications. This allows you to be accessible on your phone all the way up until you fall asleep. For those team members that actually do like to ask questions, this gives them a way to reach you. Being available for even a quick yes or no question may save you the headache from what you discover when you wake up the next morning.

This can wear you down if you are working night and day on projects. I typically have only hired outsourced team members on a short-term basis. The quicker they get their pieces done, the sooner I can move along with their code and my project.

There really is no one true solution to hiring international helpers—you just have to get into the right rhythm with each team or individual. Always consider that for every dollar that you may be saving by outsourcing your needs, you may end up spending an even greater amount of time managing their work. The question for me is: How much time spent managing them is worth the money I am saving?

CHAPTER 31

Serenity

This lesson may sound a little cliché, but it is what got me through some hard times. It's important to not get so bogged down in the day-to-day operations that you stop enjoying what you are doing. If your work becomes such a chore that you hate starting in the morning, then you know something must change. We must prevent burnout.

We all have our good and bad days, but it's paramount that you can ride the waves without letting it rip you apart. This is just a business, it's not your entire life. How many of you current business owners have been told to close your business down and head for an office job because "working for yourself is too difficult"? People who say this feel that it's much easier to just follow someone else, but we business owners like to take chances and become leaders of our own.

Even if you only work for yourself with no employees, you

must obviously have some form of leadership skills. It's very probable that many people start out with strong motivation for their businesses only to be beat down by their family and friends. They have the best intentions, but their words can often indirectly deflate your ambitions. Hear what they say, listen to their concerns, take it as constructive criticism, but choose to make your own decisions.

If someone would have told me during my down times that things can still get even worse, I may have ended my business plans and headed for an office job right then and there. Thankfully, nobody came right out and said those words to me, but I did learn that truth on my own. Clients will dry up, project proposals will fall part, and some companies just won't fully understand your abilities the way you do.

For me, these situations always seemed to happen at the same time. I learned my lessons hard, but then knew how to protect myself from letting those types of situations happen again. Don't let what others say stop you from whatever goal you wish to reach. Keep at it, fine tune how to market yourself, and you will find your niche. Understand that it won't come easy, though, and you must work hard.

Every now and then, a thought did cross my mind as to whether I should continue the fight. Those inner voices always seemed to be much stronger after a potential client walked away or a project was canceled. I would usually pamper myself with a good massage to reflect or have a good workout to release any anger. Whatever it took, I usually rebounded fairly quickly from those situations.

Some situations can be easily moved on from if your determination is strong enough. It's from the situations that you can't control that will test you more than anything else ever has. For me, it was on a personal level that I had to learn to trust in myself more than ever before. In 2013, I discovered a large mass growing on the lower side of my neck. I had a tumor about the size of half a tennis ball growing on my Thyroid, and went through a series of medical steps to have it tested out.

All of my time was slowly being eaten away by more and more medical appointments. Work took a back seat to my personal life. I was turning down projects and becoming much slower than normal in finishing the ones I was already working on. With less time for work, my financial situation started to suffer. Thankfully, the test results stated that it was not cancerous, but it was simply too large to leave in there. It was slowly growing, so I had to make the decision to have it surgically removed.

A few days after my surgery, I had my follow-up visit. I was told that the specimen results had actually come back positive for Thyroid cancer. The prior tests had not been thorough enough to see it. Hearing the words "you have cancer" gives an out-of-body experience that I can not fully explain. My mental state was instantly shattered. How could I possibly focus on any complicated projects right now with my mind wondering elsewhere? I simply didn't want to work at all.

It took me days to finally even open my software editors to

look at code. When I finally did, none of the code made any sense to me. It was like I was looking at Ancient Greek. None of this code mattered to me anymore. How could I work on this when I just had cancer removed? There was a chance I could have more cancerous cells, so they wanted to do another surgery to remove the remaining side of my thyroid. That situation seemed more important, than crunching out some code.

I had to force myself just to go through the motions of my day. My work didn't matter to me, and I could barely sleep. I would stay up most of the night reading cancer stories, currently available treatments, theories, future biotechnology topics regarding cancer treatment, and much more. This was controlling my life. Some people do try to claim that thyroid cancer is one of the safest forms of cancer to have, but this thought certainly didn't make it any easier to live with.

Within a short period of time, I was back in surgery removing the rest of my Thyroid and being scoped for any other signs of cancer. The test results from the second surgery found no other forms of cancer, so that did give me some relief. But now the fear and constant lingering thought that the cancer could come back at any time was in my head. It's like a constant reminder that I'm mortal and life as I know it could all come crashing down at any given moment. If I wasn't careful, paranoia could overrun everything I did now. What would be the point of working on meaningless software projects at this time? My mind was overwhelming me. I had to find a way to trick myself into doing my normal daily routine. So I tried to stick to my work formula and system I had built.

I started envisioning myself as a robot doing the work for myself. It may sound strange, but I saw myself as my own avatar. Like a tiny little being inside of me operating myself like a giant robot. I would tell myself the items I needed to do, throw on some soothing music, zone out, and then immerse myself in the code. I would try to deactivate my own emotional programming as soon as I would sit at my desk and then turn it back on later. I would usually re-enter into any form of shock for the rest of the night, and then start the cycle all over again the next day.

Slowly over time, my mind returned to functioning normally enough, and I was able to feel free again. An experience like that does put everything into perspective—life, how much you work, what you work on, and what are the things that truly should matter to you.

Part of my solution was to turn the fright into an informational passion. I had created bot programs that would crawl the Internet and parse the information for biotechnology trending topics. It was my way of seeing what technology advancements were emerging toward curing cancers, and then using this information for my own needs.

I decided to make this information available to day traders through a daily e-mail service with the current trending biotech topics and instant text message alerts for when clinical trial information changes throughout the day. I automated all of it.

Having instant information can mean the world to someone on a daily stock market trading schedule. I had outsmarted my fears and turned it into a passive revenue stream and an additional item to my "wheel of services".

Sometimes little jolts in our life can give us clarity to what we should be focusing our time on. The old phrase of turning lemons into lemonade just came into my mind. Life won't always go as we expect it, the same can be said for each project we work on. Each week can send us off in a new direction depending on the project. Being self-employed has taught me to always be ready for whatever comes along whether good or bad.

CHAPTER 32

One Takes, the Other Gives

I once read somewhere that Warren Buffett (I believe) said that the one thing he wished he had more of was time. You can always make more money, but you can't really buy yourself too much extra time. Doctors, exercise, attitude, environment, and eating healthy can all certainly help extend your life but not by a terribly large amount.

From a simple perspective, you are selling your life's minutes for money. That's a scary concept to consider. What percentage of your time do you work every week? How much of it is spent sleeping? How much time does that leave you to do other activities?

In the US, it seems that the work week is only growing longer and longer as people need to be more competitive to keep their jobs. Some careers in the software industry can certainly be extremely lucrative if you are willing to be nearly always working or on call.

With the emergence of smartphones, many people now have the option to never stop working. Even before heading to bed, some people are still answering messages about work. Being constantly connected makes it difficult for someone to claim that they didn't see a particular message. So if you aren't paying enough attention to your e-mails, a company may find someone else who will.

Then there are the workaholics. They choose to work themselves to the bone for the love of money. This makes me think of the phrase that goes something like "You have lots of the time, but no money. If work yourself like crazy you will have plenty of money, but no time to do anything." I have known several workaholics who had no interest in doing anything else except for the act of making money. I truly hope someday they stopped and started to enjoy the money they had been saving away.

I was once a workaholic who was always hoping to get really ahead with money. Yet something would always come along and drain my pockets for me. My health, bills, or life simply would counter punch whatever amount of money I made. One day, I tried to look back over certain periods of my life and I could barely remember anything that wasn't work-related that had happened. Most of the moments I could remember were of me sitting in front of my desk working on something.

I realized that one day, it won't matter what plans we had

made yet went unfulfilled. Life will stop, so maybe we should value the time we have right now more? I decided to take a step back and look at what I was currently working on. Was it truly worth the money I was making? If not, I had to figure out a different plan.

This certainly does not mean you should give up on life, become a pauper, and just sit on the couch counting down your minutes until it's all over. Nor am I saying that you should become a hippie, move to a beach, and give up on civilization. I am simply saying that one of the most important life lessons that I learned was to maximize my time more. I figured out what was wasting the majority of my time, what was not worth the profit, and adjusted my own formula. I decided to flip the ratio of time spent versus the money I made. So now the amount of money I would make would far outweigh the time I spent on things.

There are several books devoted to how you can better manage your daily routine. They are supposed to help you shorten your workload and leave more time for yourself. Other people I know use meditation to help calm their souls, because it helps them slice through the noise of life. These are only a couple of examples of ways you can use to challenge your own situation. I can not vouch for these books or methods, so you must determine their usefulness for yourself. Just step back and verify that you are maximizing your own time with whatever it is you would truly like to be doing with your life.

For myself, I had many other interests that were not being

fulfilled. I always wanted to travel more. For probably the first 10 years of working for myself, I barely ever traveled anywhere. Then I started going places. Sure, some of my early trips were littered with work problems, but I got better at managing things the more I traveled.

I also loved learning other spoken languages. This is when I decided to start learning Mandarin Chinese. I researched a number of languages before I ultimately decided on it. Traveling and learning this language went hand in hand, so by doing one it helped the other.

I also took up amateur winemaking, and I learned everything I could as someone without their own vineyard. I now order grapes every harvest season, and also help tend a vineyard for someone I met locally.

I personally always want to be learning new things. Whatever your interests are, just make sure you are giving yourself the time to do them. Check your workload and see how you are managing it. As a self-employed person, we are prone to overworking ourselves and never seeing the sunlight.

CHAPTER 33

Spreading Yourself Too Thin

Take a look at the more successful celebrities and business magnates and you will see that most of them have several different businesses going on at once. The obvious ones for celebrities are commercials and endorsements, but many will also have businesses that have nothing to do with their film careers. This includes restaurants, boutique shops, clothing lines, liquors, wines, beauty products, and much more.

Some, like Ashton Kutcher, have even had success with startup investing. Business magnates will often own several businesses, be heavy investors in others, and sit on boards for organizations. Every hour of every day, they could be pulling in additional income for themselves.

While us little people do not have the money that either of these groups of people may have, we should take something from these situations. None of them are relying on one thing to bring in all of their money. They are diversifying themselves with numerous passive income streams. This thought is always lingering in the back of my mind and is part of what drives me to perpetually be expanding myself into industries I may not fully understand yet. We may not be able to do these strategies on the same level as wealthier folks, but we freelancers do have the freedom to have our hands in multiple businesses at once. How can I create a better "wheel of services" that is always spinning and making money for myself?

Because of this, one issue always looms over me as I do my daily work. "Do I have enough time today to complete everything I have on my list?" If I take on too many clients at once or decide to try out a new side project idea while working on a handful of clients, I can potentially overload myself. Burnout would be devastating.

New ideas fly through my mind all day long. This can be a blessing or a curse, depending on how you want to look at it. My wife is just as crazy as I am about this. It seems like at least once a week, one of us is coming to the other with a new idea we have. Nothing is beyond our consideration; whether it is something on the Internet, something from her own career industry, a new physical product, real estate, an invention, or beyond.

The few ideas that make it to a testing phase should all be fully vetted and be given equal opportunity to prove their potential. Anyone with even the smallest amount of entrepreneurial spirit will have plenty of "great business ideas". Most of these will never succeed due to a wide range of factors. Terrible execution is what most business experts will tell you as the number one reason for failure.

I also believe that time, money, and luck all play key roles in success as well. If I had to make a guess, I would put the order of importance for these four points as: execution, timing, money, and luck. If an idea is executed correctly with the right timing, money should be easier to get. You could have solid execution, the right timing, plenty of money, yet terrible luck.

Take a currently successful idea, change a few of these factors, and then consider if it still ends up as successful. Many of the well-known successful technology companies all made it to where they are due to a little help from good timing and luck. Money is not something we all have easy access to. I've watched plenty of startups spend more time focusing on finding money than on their actual product. Because of this, their product suffered and they eventually failed.

I am always mindful of these four points when I am considering any new ideas I have. A fifth one, for me, involves the level of time I need to put into this new idea. How busy am I with my clients right now? How much time will this idea burn up when I need to be focusing on finding new clients or giving attention to one of my other passive income sources? I consider all of this when I have a new idea.

Even my hobbies are all items that may have business potential connected to them, but they too require time. Learning Mandarin Chinese could have business potential for me some day, whether it is here in the US or abroad in another country. It's a hobby that requires time every week. If I don't keep up my studying and practice, I will eventually lose everything I have learned. I must also keep it up if I wish to see continuing improvement. Amateur winemaking can be a nice conversation starter at parties, but who's to say that I may never want to take it a step further? I could get my hands on some land and start my own winery. Crazier things have happened.

After several years of letting my old film music site sit as is, I decided to pursue a redesign. I wanted something to bring the idea into the modern era. I was perfectly aware that the world had changed heavily since I first launched the site in 2001. Social media did not exist much when I launched the original version and phones certainly weren't very smart back then. There are many more websites today that offer similar services and some that have much more advanced features.

So while on the surface it seemed to be much easier to locate music to license these days, I was still hearing plenty of complaints from filmmakers who were out there looking for music. When I would speak at events, I would also hear first-hand stories from musicians having the same problems as before. During my travels to other countries, I would discuss film and music with people in their local scenes, and I was noticing that the problem really wasn't fully being handled there either. So clearly, we had stepped forward in technology, but the problem hadn't been fully solved.

After a while, I decided it was time to start focusing my extra time on creating a new version of the site since the old site would not function well on mobile phones. Additionally, the old site was only in English, but this time I went bigger with additional languages.

I decided that this site would part of a broader plan to not only help these independent filmmakers and musicians behind the scenes, but I wanted to also help promote them to the general public. So along with this new site, I launched a series of on-demand media channels full of films and music videos for people to watch on several of the streaming media devices (Roku, Android TV, Amazon Fire TV, Apple TV, and Opera TV). Many of the films currently available are from people who used the old film music site in the past to find their music, and most of the music videos were supplied by musicians who were also members of this site.

My thinking was that by connecting directly with a viewing audience, I can offer a new method of promotion to the filmmakers and musicians who use the new site. This way I can be providing support services for the artists themselves, but also a way for them to get their media in front of viewers eyes.

Once I had the streaming channels public, I was able to switch the time spent on them into other ideas. I spent it on licensing additional content for the channels or even promoting the channels. I had refreshed my film music site (a topic I love) and had added an additional form of passive income to my "wheel of services" in the process: the streaming media channels.

Us entrepreneurial types will drive ourselves crazy with so many possible ideas. Sometimes I stop and try to ask myself why I like to do these things. Is it for the love of money? Is it for the love of a challenge? Or do I just want to make a difference somehow to the world around me? I personally want a little of all of these. We all would like to have enough money to live comfortably. I personally enjoy a good challenge and there is certainly a voice deep down inside that wants to leave this planet better in some way than when I was first born into it.

One of the dangers I am always watching out for is that I will pay too much attention to these side projects and my day-to-day work will suffer. If that happens, I have become almost no different than someone with an office job who moonlights on the side. There is also a danger that on the flip side we pay too much attention to our day-to-day clients and we never devote enough time to our own ideas. Thus stopping ourselves from ever achieving more money than the max billable hours we have each week.

This is where I set aside time and goals each week for my most important side projects. I treat them as if they themselves were each a client of mine. If I do not work on them, they may fire me.

Sometimes other real clients will try to break down that mental wall by demanding your attention, and attempt to pull you away from your own project schedule. Obviously, handle their needs if this client desperately needs you now and ignoring them could hurt your standing with them. Otherwise, you have to stick to your goals. Do you want to be doing the same thing years from now? If so, then treat your ideas as nothing more than side projects for only when you have the spare time. If they mean something more to you, then you must treat them as actual clients. They must get time each week like an actual client would.

So how do we control ourselves from testing out every single idea that we have without running ourselves so thin and never completing any of them? Add up all of your personal time requirements and your day-to-day work time requirements on average for a given week. This should include any ongoing passive income businesses you have in place right now that you must spend time on. How much time does that leave for you to consider other business ideas? List out all of the ideas that you are currently testing out. Order them strictly on your own gut instinct for their potential.

What happens when you have too many of these ideas being tested at once? You should start to be able to see how little time you can give to each of them. Whenever you can't give enough time to each item, you will fail at execution for all of them. You must reorganize your items and eliminate the ones that start to appear to have the least benefit to you or appear to have lots of challenges. Your only other option is to become very good at delegating tasks to assistants whether they are virtual or in-person.

An idea, no matter how good it is, will go nowhere if you do not have enough time to see it through. Usually, the ideas that will eat up the largest amount of my time and money will get put on hold or canceled first. Understand that you are just one person. Spot the ideas that even with a handful of paid assistants - will take up too much of your time and remove them.

Understand that someone out there has more than likely also thought of the same idea as you. This can actually be a good thing. Seek out information about their business and study how it was set up. Is it also just one person with some assistants? Or is it a full company with employees? Sometimes, seeing how your future competition is structured can help you gauge a few things. It can help you see what someone else felt was necessary to make that same idea flourish.

What you felt would require you and a virtual assistant, they may have felt would take an entire office of 10 people. Who is right in this situation? Take a step back and try to consider all aspects of your idea. Are you forgetting something that they considered?

Study how successful their business seems. Do their social media pages seem busy? Are people discussing the business heavily on the Internet? Consider that the level of buzz around their business may be the result of terrible execution. If so, would you be able to do it better?

How likely would it be that you could compete with them? Are you going to be able to spend the time and money to execute a solid plan of competition? These are all questions you should be asking yourself before pursuing an idea that someone else has already executed.

Considering that we only have so much time every day to pursue our ideas, so it's important to not be too stubborn. You do not want an another idea fail because you are too busy competing against someone else who has a better execution plan than you for your current idea.

Many business books and experts will tell you that competition is good, and that having competitors just proves that the idea is something people are interested in. I don't always agree with these business experts myself. Some ideas simply will make more profit when they control a niche.

Ultimately, for me, the ideas that resonate enough that I continue on with them must hit the sweet spot between all five of the main points I mentioned before. It must also not burn up too much of my time from other items. Building and marketing this one idea must also not drain my bank account too heavily. The timing must appear to be right. My gut instinct on the idea must be high enough that it makes me feel that the probability of success is good. And finally, I consider how well thought-out my plan of execution is.

A final factor that may help me make a choice is whether it's a topic I truly enjoy. Loving what you do will usually make you strive harder for success, but some successful people do conduct businesses they really have no interest in. While I could probably do this too, I know I work harder when I enjoy what it is that I am working on.

If I feel these items are all met to my own level of

requirements, I will then take a step back from it for a few days or a week. Am I confident enough in this idea to commit all of these resources to it? Will it absorb so much of my resources that everything else may suffer?

Only you will know the correct answer to these questions. You must never become complacent to the sunk time and cost on an idea, though. If after a certain period of time you can see that nothing is coming out of it, do not be afraid to end things. Move on to your next big idea.

CHAPTER 34

Mastering Payment Options

When I first started my business, I knew of only one way to get money sent to me from a client. I would send an invoice and they would mail me a check within a short period of time. This sounded simple enough. Boy, was I naive. I've previously mentioned some of my troubles already about how sometimes invoices that were emailed have magically gone missing.

Clients may sometimes claim that they never saw it. Weeks later, you may still be fighting with them just to get a check in the mail. So I would re-send the invoice, now suddenly they have received this version, and will finally send me a check "soon". It's already been a few weeks since I sent the first invoice, but in their mind this newly received version restarts the 30-day payment clock all over.

So theoretically, I am supposed to sit around for another number of weeks waiting for my money to come in. To top this all off, some will then forget to throw it in the mail even after they said they would. Whether this is an attached file to an e-mail or just a link to an online invoice, these types of people will find a way to get out of paying you as long as possible. You try to be as patient as possible, and understand human error does occur. Eventually this patience gets smaller and smaller with each time it happens to you.

Something had to change. Using the mail was simply too slow. I already had a merchant account for my film music site, so I decided to offer my day-to-day clients the ability to pay by credit card. I didn't necessarily like this idea since I would lose a cut of my money to merchant fees.

What did I hate more, though? Going for months while waiting on money or getting my money now minus the merchant fees? I would take the money now option. This allowed me to catch a few clients who were clearly just trying to come up with excuses to delay paying me longer. Having them on the phone made it easy to receive credit card numbers instantly.

I did eventually start to charge a small extra amount of money on my invoices for those clients who were set up to automatically allow me to charge their credit cards. This way, I would not lose extra money on the merchant fees since they themselves were covering it for me. Merchant accounts were very pricey in those days, though, because you had to pay a monthly fee as well as lose a percentage of your money from each transaction. The ease and speed of receiving my money were what continued to push me to use this method, though.

This worked for a while, but some invoices were too large to charge and my merchant company started rejecting some of my transactions. I also accepted Paypal for my film music site and from my day-to-day clients. This had the same problem as the credit card merchant, though: high fees. I had also heard stories about how Paypal was known to always side with a customer in regards to reversing charges.

As a service provider, all it would take was for a client to click on a link to reverse their payment to me and I was basically screwed out of this money. I never had this happen personally, but I do know other independents who did.

Eventually, I reverted back to just taking payments the old-fashioned way of receiving a check by mail. Thankfully, today there are other methods that have now become available.

Most of the major banks all have their own private direct payment networks now. For a while, one of my clients liked to send their payments using Chase Quickpay, while another liked to send it via a similar method using Wells Fargo's Surepay. If you use a credit union as your primary bank, most of the major banks can transfer money to each other and credit unions using the clearXchange network.

The client could send money to you, for example, using the previously mentioned Wells Fargo Surepay. They just put in your e-mail address and the amount they wish to send you, but you must have this same e-mail address already registered on the clearXchange network. Make sure you have entered your personal bank routing and account numbers into your clearXchange account. Now, if anyone ever sends money to your e-mail address again using one of the major bank services, clearXchange will pick it up and automatically direct deposit your money into the credit union account you previously registered. It's good because you don't have to do any extra steps every time a payment is sent to you. An e-mail will be sent to your address on file so that you know something is going on.

Another service that some clients like to use is called Square Cash. It is fairly similar to the ones mentioned above, but it is a standalone service. What sets it above the others is that is has a very easy to understand mobile phone application. At the time I was writing this, Square Cash is free to send money if it is for personal use, but for business transactions there is a small fee.

Some clients like to use variations of the old direct deposit methods. One paid service I am familiar with is called Paymo. It's a time-tracking management service and a way to manage paying your team. So you can input your staff and their billable hours into the system.

Employees have the option of either starting a time clock on their phone while they are working through the Paymo app or they can manually enter their hours themselves later on. If you have previously entered a pay rate for each of your staff, Paymo will automatically generate the amount it should pay them on a monthly basis.

You can either approve these amounts or change them. Then it handles depositing the money into their bank accounts. If you are thinking of hiring a staff of developers to help you with your projects, this type of service may certainly be of help to you.

Many of the freelancing websites have their own style of escrow services. This forces the client to deposit money into the website before you should start working on their project. It's supposed to protect you from doing work and never getting paid. It's a good idea in theory, but I have heard several horror stories from other developers about the issues they have had with these types of services.

First and foremost, these sites want to make money. They are businesses after all. They usually charge the project poster a small percentage fee for posting their project. Then the website will charge the project poster another percentage fee when they are depositing money for the winning bidder. And then finally, they will also charge a percentage commission fee from the developer's payment. Many of these freelancing sites only deposit into Paypal or a US bank account. If you need to convert the money from US currency into your own local currency, there may also be additional fees.

Another major concern developers have with these websites is that sometimes the client may try to get out of paying you for your work. When this happens, you will have to enter into payment arbitration. Both you and the client will tell your sides of the story to the website arbitration team. Then it is up to this arbitration team to decide what the solution is. From the stories I hear, they tend to side more often with the client, regardless of the situation.

My only theory on this is that the clients are the ones bringing new money to the freelancing website. They are the ones posting projects, therefore they are creating the money flow. The fact is that there are simply more of you developers wanting to make money than the people posting new projects. I guess I see the business logic behind this, but it's still hard to believe. I, personally, can not say whether one way or other is truly the case. I have never been through a situation like this before myself.

The good news is that in this day and age, there are plenty of options for direct payments between people in different countries. A more controversial form of payment from country to country is by using one of the many cryptocurrencies. Bitcoin, one of the first available, is still the most widely used and possibly most trusted of them all. Bitcoin was first introduced in 2008 and then took several years to reach a wider audience.

The general idea behind Bitcoin and its cryptocurrency cousins is that payments are made directly between you and the person you wish to send money to. Each person's computer generates payment keys that look like a long string of alphabet soup sprinkled with some numbers.

When someone sends you money, Bitcoin utilizes peer-to-peer software that encrypts the transactions and syncs them across a network until it reaches your computer. All transactions are verified using a network of nodes around the world. All of this technology comes together into what is called a blockchain. It's a way to allow anonymous people around the world to send money to each other by just using a computer. Each transaction charges an extremely tiny amount of money to send out.

In some countries, businesses accepting Bitcoin as a form of payment have become more popular than they are here in the US. Just as Bitcoin seemed to be gaining in popularity, the US government teamed up with most of the major banks to slow it down. Since cryptocurrencies aid people in transacting money anonymously, the US government wanted to stop it in its tracks. The general discussion was that terrorists, drug sellers, and other illegal activities were using it to pass money between each other without the government being able to stop it.

When you receive Bitcoin, your "coins" are kept inside an encrypted folder on the computer you have your Bitcoin application on. If that computer crashes or you delete the folder, you lose your coins. There is no backup. So, some people started creating websites that were meant to allow you to hold your coins online, just like you can login to your bank account. The problem was, if someone gained access to your account, your coins could be actually stolen.

They are not insured by any agency in case your coins are stolen, and these websites themselves could be hacked and your coins may be stolen. The websites could still list that your coins are there, but in reality the coins were stolen long ago from this web server. This has sadly happened a few times, and people have lost large amounts of coins worth an extremely massive amount of money. In some cases, these hacks were actually inside jobs—the companies themselves were stealing people's coins.

It all started sounding like a virtual Wild Wild West where standalone banks in newly settled towns were being robbed and completely emptied. No FDIC or similar insured banking services were around to get people's money back.

The few transactions I have done with Bitcoin went very smoothly. The developers I worked with had no issues receiving their coins either. I still offer it to some of the developers I work with, but it seems the interest in it has faded over the last couple of years.

Some developers and companies I work with internationally still prefer the more common forms of payments available for years. One group of developers I work with prefers wire transfers. We had also previously used a service similar to Square Cash called Payoneer, but this team decided that they liked wire transfers better.

Wire transfers haven't changed much over the years, but it is important to get the information correct on your transfer documents. Thankfully, many of the larger banks now offer a way for you to create wire transfers directly through their websites. I was growing tired of having to walk into a physical bank and then sit with a teller as they filled out all of the information for me. This process seemed very out of date considering what other options we have now.

Besides wire transfers, some international developers I have worked with prefer Western Union or MoneyGram. While you can do these through their websites and on your phone at your home, I have learned that these companies do not always approve your payments this way. If you want to pay someone located in a country that may be deemed questionable, more often than not these companies will deny your payment. You will need to physically go to a business that offers their services, and set up the payment this way. By doing this, it's supposed to prove you are a real human and really want to send your money to this other person.

This happened to me once. I was looking for new films to license for my streaming media channels. A filmmaker from Uganda was referred to me by another filmmaker that I had already worked with. The Ugandan filmmaker and I agreed on a set price for his films, and now I needed to pay him. But how? He wasn't interested in Bitcoin. None of the other methods seemed to be a possibility. So we agreed on one of these money transfer services. I tried to send the payment through that service's website. I received a response that I needed call their headquarters in order to complete the transaction.

During this call, it fully hit me: these people thought I was becoming a victim of one of those African e-mail scams. I explained my situation to the person on the phone, but I could tell he was completely lost with what I was doing. I was put on hold as he consulted with his supervisor. After a long pause, he came back to say my transaction was denied. I would need to go into a local drug store down the street and complete the transaction from this service's kiosk. I refrained from getting angry and just walked to the store.

The kiosk was nothing more than a red telephone that called the same customer service line. Now I had to spell out the Ugandan filmmaker's name over the phone and say everything to this person instead of being able to type it out. I had to hope that this person got everything correct. Once it was done, I hung up the phone, and had to pay my money to the drug store clerk. There was no lengthy questions, no sense of shame that I was being scammed, but it seemed like massive overkill just to send a small amount of money to another country.

The silver lining to sending this payment from the store kiosk was that the final price was a few dollars cheaper than it was online. The few dollars I saved was not enough to make up for the extra amounts of time and hoops I had to jump through just to send real money. It would be great if the US could catch up to some of the payment methods other countries have already been able to offer.

CHAPTER 35

Have a Plan for Your Future

Where do you go from here? What's your end game? Do you see yourself working with clients like this for the next 20 years? Or are you hoping to take one of your side projects to the next level?

Many of my generation were born with the idea that a full career path was the right way to go. That each of us must go to college, find a job, get married, have children, and work at that same company until we retire. We were lead to believe that this planned out life offers the best stability and a level of safety until our dying day.

Many of us now see that this way of life no longer offers the stability it may have once offered. Yes, office jobs do offer ways to help you have a safer bet for the future with their 401(k) plans, pensions, and saving accounts. Yet these are not without their own concerns. Stock markets can tumble, pensions may vanish, and savings accounts often shrink from inflation.

I've heard enough horror stories (including some from people I personally know) about once proud companies now bankrupt with retired people who have lost all of their guaranteed pensions. It seems to me that no office employee's financial future is as safe as it was years ago.

Being on your own as a freelancer can be hard at times, especially if you haven't pushed hard enough to land the right clients. This can be a serious long-term issue, and you may not have the financial security you were hoping to have.

Unfortunately, we also age, so it is likely that we cannot work the same career our entire lives. Our own physical hardware is slowly giving out on us. I know without any doubt that I simply do not have the same level of energy I had 20 years ago. I may be wiser and mentally stronger now, but I couldn't beat an 18-year-old version of myself in a foot race.

We must always be preparing for the next stage of our lives whether we are salaried or an independent. As freelancers, we must understand that the general markets will shift, and our techniques for landing clients will slowly stop working. Following the trends and altering our main focus can help prolong us for a while, but eventually, those too will stop being effective.

We must have a plan for that period of our life. Can a freelancer truly retire? If so, when exactly is the right time? What kind of a career should we do in the next phase of our lives? All of these questions differ for each of us. So what about my own plans? What direction am I heading? I think I will stop my software consulting business once I no longer have any desire to learn new coding techniques. Sure, I will shift my roles over time, and may start to rely more heavily on a support team. Exactly when I will do that is not known to me yet. One day, I will just know I guess.

I believe that I have wanted to run a business as far back as I can remember. Even from a young age, I enjoyed playing video games like "Lemonade Stand" which allowed me to practice my business-building skills. I even remember myself and a friend trying to sell crayon drawings and crafts to our classmates in grade school.

Once I hit my teen years and the Internet was taking off, I wrote my first short story and made it available for people to buy online. Several people who I did not know purchased it from across the US. It wasn't a huge amount by any means, but it was still fun to print each copy out and mail them to a stranger. I guess business is just in my blood.

What about the distant future, where do I see myself in 20 years? Wherever my life allows me to be. That's the beauty of being my own boss. Working wherever I want, on whatever I want. I can say for certain that I know where I won't be: places that the experiences in this book have taught me to never go back to. Many of my side project ideas are for my future because I know that I can't always rely on being a freelance software consultant.

If I have no plan, I may have to set up my own lemonade stand, become a department store door-greeter, or who knows what else in order to pay my bills. This is why I test my ideas now while I still have the financial security, so that I can be planting the seeds of these ideas now in order to protect myself from tomorrow.

So here we are at the end of my book. I hope that you have found something of value from the experiences I have endured. There were plenty of other stories to tell, but the ones I included in here were the ones that had the most impact on my life.

If I had to sum up my best advice, it would be the following: Stand your ground, fail enough times to make yourself smarter, learn how to maximize your time to make more money, find a good work and life balance, take nothing personal from business dealings, double whatever you are charging right now, say "No" more often, and reflect on all of your mistakes.

Most importantly, learn from the mistakes of others, like me.

Lessons Learned While Freelancing

#1: Ignore the distractions and focus on your goals

#2: Clients may use fake personalities on the Internet

#3: Learn how not to run a business

#4: Work will be feast or famine

#5: Prepare a backup plan

#6: Create passive incomes

#7: Be willing to open your mind

#8: Remember your supporters

#9: Be prepared to keep your work promises

#10: Do not rely on just one client

#11: Maintain a good health care plan

#12: A project is not yours until you sign the contract

#13: Work will invade your vacations

#14: Learn how to reinvent yourself or become obsolete

#15: Accept that you may lose money

#16: Break out of your introverted shell

#17: Work smarter, not harder

#18: Regulate your work flow with the 80/20 rule

#19: Discover your niche to get better clients

#20: Expect to go without pay for months at a time

#21: Startups are high risk, high reward

#22: Create a work routine and stick to it

#23: Establish business hours and abide by them

#24: Be cautious of clients who say their project will be easy

#25: Learn to control clients that blame you for everything

#26: Master how to assist under-experienced clients

#27: Try to slow down rush projects

#28: Become opportunistic and play to the trends

#29: Use freelancing websites to your advantage

#30: Accept outsourcing for what it is and let it help you

#31: Accept your growths and the things you can not change

#32: Time is more important than money

#33: Do not spread yourself too thin

#34: Save money by understanding your payment options

#35: Have a plan for your future

About the Author

Ryan Vinson has been a software engineer for over 20 years and an independent consultant for 15 years. He has had an unquenchable thirst for knowledge and curiosity about the world since he was a little boy. In his spare time, he is an amateur winemaker, enjoys studying history, and volunteers at an animal rescue. He lives in Los Angeles, California with his wife Seak and cat Isabella.

For additional information, visit:

www.DisregardedEntityBook.com

www.RyanVinson.com